T0308219

EVERYTHING YOU NEED TO KNOW ABOUT THE ULURU STATEMENT FROM THE HEART

MEGAN DAVIS is the Balnaves Chair in Constitutional Law, Director of the Indigenous Law Centre at UNSW Law and Pro Vice Chancellor at UNSW. She is the leading constitutional lawyer on Indigenous constitutional recognition and was a member of the Prime Minister's Referendum Council and the Prime Minister's Expert Panel on Constitutional Recognition. She is a United Nations expert based in the UN Human Rights Council, Geneva and formerly UN New York. She is a Cobble Cobble woman from south-west Queensland.

GEORGE WILLIAMS AO is the Anthony Mason Professor and a Scientia Professor, as well as a Deputy Vice Chancellor, at UNSW. He has published books including *Australian Constitutional Law and Theory*, *The Oxford Companion to the High Court of Australia* and *Human Rights Under the Australian Constitution*. He has appeared as a barrister in the High Court of Australia and is a columnist for *The Australian*.

MEGAN DAVIS &
GEORGE WILLIAMS

EVERYTHING YOU NEED TO KNOW ABOUT THE ULURU STATEMENT FROM THE HEART

UNSW PRESS

A UNSW Press book

Published by
NewSouth Publishing
University of New South Wales Press Ltd
University of New South Wales
Sydney NSW 2052
AUSTRALIA
newsouthpublishing.com

First published 2021

10 9 8 7 6 5 4 3 2 1

ISBN 9781742237404 (paperback)
9781742245300 (ebook)
9781742249865 (ePDF)

NATIONAL LIBRARY OF AUSTRALIA
A catalogue record for this book is available from the National Library of Australia

Cover design Luke Causby, Blue Cork
Cover image Uluru, after the ceremony to mark the permanent closure of the climb in 2019 (photograph by Jimmy Widders Hunt)
Internal design Josephine Pajor-Markus

UNSW
SYDNEY

CONTENTS

INTRODUCTION

Recognition of Aboriginal and Torres Strait Islander peoples in the Australian Constitution has attracted national attention for decades. What is all the fuss about? Why have so many people championed the idea? And how do Indigenous peoples want to be recognised in the Constitution?

The final question was answered at an historic gathering of Aboriginal and Torres Strait Islander peoples at Uluru in 2017. A statement was issued to the Australian people on what constitutional recognition should include. The Uluru Statement from the Heart called for a First Nations 'Voice' to Parliament protected by the Constitution and a subsequent process of agreement-making and truth-telling. This law reform proposal is popularly referred to as Voice, Treaty, Truth.

This call for constitutional reform has a long history in Indigenous communities. One example is Cherbourg in south-western Queensland. Cherbourg was set up by the Salvation Army in 1899 and became a settlement in 1904 under Queensland's *Aboriginals Protection and Restrictions of the Sale of Opium Act 1897*.

Cherbourg has conducted discussions on the Constitution on the verandah of the old Ration Shed, the dwelling where small rations of tea, salt, sugar, peas, porridge and flour were given out weekly until 1968.

The symbolism was obvious. In 1901, as Australia embarked on its journey as a new nation with a new Constitution, Aboriginal people were forcibly removed from their country and placed on reserves and missions. Federation meant a loss of rights and freedom for Aboriginal people as they bore the burden of discrimination imposed by law. They were denied the vote, had their children removed, were prevented from marrying, were told where they could live and had their wages confiscated. But a year after a campaign led by many voices from within Cherbourg led to the 1967 referendum that deleted discriminatory references to Aboriginal people from the Constitution, the Ration Shed was closed. To Cherbourg residents, this illustrated the power of the Constitution.

Aunty Beryl Gambrill – who was arrested for protesting in 1967 in support of the referendum – participated again in 2011 at age 80 in national discussions about constitutional change. She made a submission on the verandah of the Ration Shed, handwritten in pencil, that recognition is 'important to us' and that it should happen 'as soon as possible'.[1] One year later she passed away. Her contribution to equal rights and the community at large was so significant that a condolence motion was passed in the Queensland Parliament.

Some say urgent things are needed in the area of Aboriginal policy and disadvantage, so why focus on constitutional change? Aunty Beryl is an excellent example of why; Aboriginal and Torres Strait Islander peoples have themselves identified the need for this reform. They have argued for change since the early years after Federation, in response to their first-hand experience of how the Constitution has impacted negatively on their lives.

They have done so because the Constitution excluded them from the political settlement that brought about the new Australian nation. Rather than being treated as equal citizens, they were cast as a 'dying race' not expected to survive British settlement. They were described as a 'problem' and as a people lacking any future in the nation. This was reflected in the fact that they were immediately denied the vote in federal elections and the Constitution said they could not be included in counts of the Australian population.

The Constitution can seem distant from people's lives, but it is always there, in the background, shaping the work of parliaments, governments and courts. The Constitution influences our lives from day-to-day, as we saw during the Coronavirus pandemic as the Commonwealth worked with the states to safeguard the community. The Constitution has a long-term, profound effect on the direction of the nation and its laws. The Constitution is the 'rule book' for the nation that:

- creates power in Australian society (and so determines who can do what and to whom);
- establishes the legitimacy of, and relationships between, people and institutions; and
- recognises values and national aspirations.

In each of these ways, the Constitution affects Aboriginal and Torres Strait Islander peoples and their place within the community.

The advocacy of Aboriginal and Torres Strait Islander peoples culminated in a successful referendum in 1967. Since then, many people – including a long list of Aboriginal people and Torres Strait Islanders and successive prime ministers from Paul Keating and John Howard onwards – have agitated for further change. These calls emerged as it became clear that the 1967 referendum had left unfinished business.

The 1967 referendum deleted discriminatory references to Aboriginal people but put nothing in their place. Torres Strait Islanders have never been referred to in the Constitution at all. As a result, rather than recognising Indigenous people, the referendum left a silence at the heart of the Constitution. Today, the document reflects Australia's history of British settlement but fails to acknowledge the much longer occupation of the continent by Aboriginal and Torres Strait Islander peoples. It is as if this history does not matter and is not part of the nation's story.

The 1967 referendum also did not deal with other issues of importance to Indigenous peoples. These include the settlement of differences through the making of treaties and the need to have a say on laws that affect Indigenous peoples. In bypassing these and other issues, the 1967 referendum failed to make structural changes to improve the relationship between the state and Indigenous peoples.

Some people find it hard to see why these issues should be tackled when so much else needs to be done. The evidence time and time again illustrates the disadvantage Aboriginal and Torres Strait Islander peoples experience and how this manifests in poor life expectancy and unemployment. One of the ways of addressing this is constitutional recognition.

Overcoming disadvantage requires multiple approaches. Recognition and ensuring an Indigenous Voice to Parliament are some of the things that could accelerate improvement.

Constitutional change of this kind could have broad, positive effects that extend far beyond the law. For example, the referendum could unite Australians around a sense of their shared history which, for the first time in the Constitution, would include the long habitation of the continent by Aboriginal and Torres Strait Islander peoples. This is reflected in the fact that the Uluru Statement from the Heart was issued as an 'invitation' to the Australian people to work with First Nations peoples on a journey that would repeat what was done in unity in 1967. The invitation explained why constitutional change is so integral to improving the situation of Indigenous peoples in Australia.

Constitutional recognition could also have positive health effects. Research on the social determinants of health shows how legal discrimination and exclusion can have a negative impact on mental and physical wellbeing. Indeed, it is hard to underestimate the emotional and other costs of being cast as an outsider in your own land. Experts have recognised this. For example, the Royal Australian and New Zealand College of Psychiatrists notes:

> The lack of acknowledgement of a people's existence in a country's constitution has a major impact on their sense of identity and value within the community, and perpetuates discrimination and prejudice which further erodes the hope of Indigenous people. There is an association with socioeconomic disadvantage and subsequent higher rates of mental illness, physical illness and incarceration.

> Recognition in the Constitution would have a positive effect on the self-esteem of Indigenous Australians and reinforce their pride in their culture and history. It would make a real difference to the lives of Indigenous Australians, and is an important step to support and improve the lives and mental health of Indigenous Australians.[2]

Examples from other countries such as Canada, New Zealand and the United States highlight how the right legal settings can produce better health outcomes. The hope is that changing the Australian Constitution to recognise Aboriginal and Torres Strait Islander peoples will contribute in the same way.

Australians may soon vote in a referendum on whether to change the Constitution to recognise Aboriginal and Torres Strait Islander peoples. Despite this, few people understand what is being proposed. Our goal in this book is to set out what people need to know to understand our nation's journey towards constitutional recognition. This means exploring where the Constitution came from, and the role Indigenous peoples played in its drafting.

We also examine how the Constitution was altered in 1967, and why that referendum has led to calls for further change today. An important focus is the Uluru Statement and its call for a constitutionally enshrined voice to Parliament. We conclude by setting out how a referendum to achieve that reform can be won.

This book is uniquely placed as the first comprehensive consideration of Indigenous constitutional recognition in Australia and in particular includes the work of the Referendum Council and the Uluru Statement from the Heart. Megan Davis, the first author of this book, was a member of the Referendum Council and designed the regional dialogue method that led to the consensus at Uluru on 26 May 2017. She read the Uluru Statement from the Heart to the national convention and then the Australian public for the first time. Davis examined constitutional change processes including citizen conventions and deliberative democracy and more importantly Indigenous constitutional change processes globally and drew upon the experience of those working with communities including Aunty Pat Anderson, Noel Pearson, Patrick Dodson, Dalassa Yorkston, Galarrwuy Yunupingu and many others who work and live in Aboriginal and Torres Strait Islander communities to design the process.

George Williams, the second author, has also been involved with many of the contemporary events described in this book in his work as a constitutional lawyer. As a barrister he appeared for the Ngarrindjeri women in the Hindmarsh Island Bridge Case in 1998 and has provided support and advice on matters including the making of treaties and constitutional recognition to parliaments and organisations such as land councils, the National Congress of Australia's First Peoples, ATSIC and the Council for Aboriginal Reconciliation. He has also written widely and been engaged in many debates about constitutional change in Australia.

TIMELINE

Since time immemorial Aboriginal and Torres Strait Islander peoples have lived on the land now known as Australia for at least 60 000 years.

1770 Captain James Cook claims the land now known as Australia.

1788 Captain Arthur Phillip and the First Fleet arrive at Botany Bay.

1846 Exiled Tasmanian Aboriginal people on Flinders Island petition Queen Victoria about agreement made with Colonel Arthur.

1881 Petition from residents of Maloga mission (Yorta Yorta) to NSW Governor seeking land grants (residents soon after moved to Cummergunja reserve).

1886 William Barak wrote from Coranderrk: 'We should be free like the White Population there is only few Blacks now rem[a]ining in Victoria ... and we Blacks of Aboriginal Blood, wish to have now freedom for all our life time'.

1890s Debates over a federal Constitution: Aboriginal people not involved and barely mentioned in Conventions.

1891 The first Constitutional Convention is held in Sydney.

1897–98 Constitutional Conventions are held in Adelaide, Sydney and Melbourne.

1901 Australia becomes a nation when the Constitution of Australia comes into force.

1912 David Unaipon called for Narrandjeri autonomy over the Point Macleay reserve.

1926 Unaipon called for the establishment of an Aboriginal state.

1924 The Australian Aboriginal Progressive Association (AAPA) is formed in Sydney.

1927 Fred Maynard calls for abolition of protection and control of Aboriginal affairs.

1933 William Cooper petitions the King seeking intervention including representation in federal Parliament. The Commonwealth did not send it on to the King. Burraga Joe Anderson calls for Indigenous representation in the federal Parliament.

1934 David Unaipon urged Commonwealth to take over Aboriginal affairs from the States.

1936 Torres Strait Maritime strike which directly leads to Qld government establishing Island councils which gave them political representation and authority and some power.

1937 Yorta Yorta man William Cooper petitions King George VI for representation in Parliament.

1938 The Australian Aborigines' League and the Aborigines Progressive Association hold a 'Day of Mourning', calling for Commonwealth control of Indigenous affairs and a national policy.

1949 Secretary of Australia Aborigines League Doug Nicholls wrote to Prime Minister Chifley seeking representation of Aboriginal people in the Federal Parliament.

1958 The Federal Council for Aboriginal Advancement is created (renamed in 1964 as the Federal Council for the Advancement of Aborigines and Torres Strait Islanders).

1962 Indigenous Australians granted the right to vote in federal elections.

1963 The Yolngu Nation send the Yirrkala Bark Petitions to the Parliament objecting to the excision of land from their reserve for mining. They were not consulted and 'fear their needs and interests will be completely ignored as they have been ignored in the past'.

1966 Vincent Lingiari and Dexter Daniels led their people in a walk-off at Wave Hill station, NT and fight for wages, land rights and self-determination.

1967 A referendum is successfully held to grant legislative power over Aboriginal people to the federal Parliament to include Aboriginal people in the census. This is the highest 'Yes' vote in Australian history.

1971 The Federal Court rules against Yolngu land rights claim in the first significant land rights case in Australia.

1972 The Larrakia Petition is signed by hundreds of Indigenous people, calling for land rights and political representation.

1973 National Aboriginal Consultative Committee (NACC) established and later replaced in 1977 with the National Aboriginal Conference (NAC).

1973 The Whitlam government establishes a royal commission to examine ways to recognise Aboriginal land rights.

1975 *Racial Discrimination Act* enacted by the federal Parliament.

1976 Commonwealth used its constitutional power to legislate land rights in Territory. This starts the push to use the power from the 1967 referendum to create national land rights.

1977 The Fraser government creates the National Aboriginal Conference.

1979 National Aboriginal Conference calls for a treaty to be negotiated between Aboriginal people and the Commonwealth following nationwide consultations with Aboriginal and Torres Strait Islander communities.

1983 Senate Standing Committee on Legal and Constitutional Affairs hands down its report *Two Hundred Years Later* … which recommends the government consider a treaty in consultation with Aboriginal peoples. The committee also recommends the insertion into the Constitution of a provision 'which would confer a broad power on the Commonwealth to enter into a compact with representatives of the Aboriginal people'.

1988 A second bark petition is presented to Prime Minister Bob Hawke by Galarrwuy Yunupingu. The Barunga Statement calls for recognition of Aboriginal rights and for a national elected Aboriginal and Islander organisation to oversee Aboriginal and Islander affairs, and for the Commonwealth to negotiate a treaty.

1989 The Federal Parliament creates a new independent statutory body, the Aboriginal and Torres Strait Islander Commission (ATSIC), after an extensive consultation period including 500 meetings with 14 500 people.

1991 Australia commences a decade of statutory 'reconciliation', with the federal Parliament enacting a law establishing the Council for Aboriginal Reconciliation.

1992 The High Court hands down the *Mabo* case, in which it recognises native title and rejects the idea that Australia was *terra nullius*, or no man's land, at the time of British settlement. Prime Minister Paul Keating makes the Redfern Speech, acknowledging the history of dispossession in Australia.

1993 Keating legislates native title into law. After months of pressure, protest and tough negotiations, the Act goes through Parliament. Keating also promises compensation where native title cannot deliver by creating a land fund and a social justice package.

1995 An ATSIC Committee delivers the *Recognition, Rights and Reform* report, which is the repair element of the Mabo settlement. It affirms community aspirations to constitutional recognition in light of *Mabo*. The social justice package remains unimplemented.

1997 Human Rights and Equal Opportunity Commission tables the *Bringing Them Home* report, which examines the former practice of separating Aboriginal and Torres Strait Islander children from their families. The report recommends an official government apology to the Stolen Generations. Prime Minister John Howard refuses to provide this.

1998 The High Court of Australia hands down the *Hindmarsh Island Bridge* decision, which leaves open the possibility that section 51(xxvi) of the Constitution can be used by the Commonwealth to impose racially discriminatory laws upon Aboriginal people.

1999 Australia holds a referendum to decide whether to become a republic, and also on whether to adopt a new preamble to the Constitution which acknowledges Aboriginal and Torres Strait Islander peoples. Howard went ahead with wording that ATSIC and the land councils rejected. It was purely a symbolic mention honouring Indigenous people combined with a vote on the republic. The Australian people rejected both proposals.

2000 The Council for Aboriginal Reconciliation delivers its *Australian Declaration towards Reconciliation* and the *Roadmap for Reconciliation*. The report reinforces Aboriginal and Torres Strait Islander aspirations for a treaty and constitutional change.

2005 Parliament formally abolishes ATSIC.

2007 Days prior to the federal election, Prime Minister John Howard announces the government's intention to hold a referendum to symbolically recognise Aboriginal and Torres Strait Islander peoples in a new preamble to the Constitution.

2008 Prime Minister Kevin Rudd presents the Apology to the Stolen Generations. The Australia 2020 Summit is held, with the final report noting the 'strong view that recognition of Aboriginal and Torres Strait Islander peoples' rights needs to be included in the body of the Constitution, not just in the Preamble'. The Prime Minister is presented with a Statement of Intent from Yolngu and Bininj Leaders, who express their desire for constitutional protection for traditional land and cultural rights.

2010 Prime Minister Julia Gillard establishes the Expert Panel on the Recognition of Aboriginal and Torres Strait Islander Peoples in the Constitution.

2012 The Expert Panel hands down its report. There is strong support for constitutional recognition. The panel recommends a new race power with words of recognition, removing the remaining clauses that enable racial discrimination and a non-discrimination clause.

2013 The Gillard government, with support from the Opposition, passes the *Aboriginal and Torres Strait Islander Peoples Recognition Act 2013, to* provide an interim form of recognition of Aboriginal people.

2014 Parliament forms a joint select parliamentary committee, chaired by Senators Ken Wyatt and Nova Peris, to advance the work of the Expert Panel.

2015 Indigenous Leaders meet with Prime Minister Malcolm Turnbull and Opposition Leader Bill Shorten at Kirribilli House and issue the Kirribilli Statement. In response, the Prime Minister and Opposition Leader establish the Referendum Council.

2016–17 The Referendum Council runs 13 First Nations Regional Dialogues to discuss options for constitutional reform, and to ensure that Aboriginal decision-making is at the heart of the reform process.

2017 The National Constitutional Convention is held at Uluru and the process ratifies the decision making of the Regional Dialogues. The Uluru Statement from the Heart is issued to the Australian people. This calls for a constitutionally entrenched First Nations Voice to Parliament, and a Makarrata commission to oversee a process of treaty-making and truth-telling. The Referendum Council hands down its final report, which endorses the Uluru Statement from the Heart and its call for Voice, Treaty and Truth. The Turnbull government rejects the call for a Voice to Parliament.

2018 A Joint Select Committee of Parliament to consider the work of the Referendum Council, chaired by Senators Patrick Dodson and Julian Leeser, undertakes its work. In its final report, it finds the Voice is the only viable recognition proposal and recommends that the government 'initiate a process of co-design [of the Voice] with Aboriginal and Torres Strait Islander peoples'.

2019 Minister for Indigenous Australians, Ken Wyatt, announces a 'co-design' process to determine the structure and functions of the Voice.

2021 The interim report on the Indigenous Voice Proposal is released. Stage two of the 'co-design' process commences, inviting feedback on the proposals on the design of the Voice.

1

MAKING THE CONSTITUTION

Aboriginal and Torres Strait Islander peoples have lived on the Australian continent and its islands for more than 60 000 years. They are recognised as having the oldest continuous culture on the planet. They speak of their ancestors as travellers of the continent during the Creation. The Creation forms the basis of Aboriginal law, which is passed down through song, dance, rock and sand painting, language and oral explanations of myth. Before the arrival of the British, Aboriginal and Torres Strait Islander society included sophisticated political, social and cultural organisation, including trading networks and a complex system of governance, justice and decision-making. They were custodians of the 'biggest estate on earth', caring for 7.7 million square kilometres of land, which their law prescribed that they leave 'as they found it'.[1]

Several European explorers reached the Australian coast, but it was not until Captain James Cook of England in 1770 that any sought to claim the land. Cook arrived on the east coast of Australia with the following instructions from the British Navy: 'You are also, with the consent of the natives, to take possession of Convenient Situations in the Country in the Name of the King of Great Britain'.[2] Cook was not to take the lands by force. He had been told by James Douglas, President of the Royal Society sponsoring the scientific voyage, that if any people were encountered, they were 'in the strictest sense of the word, the legal possessors of the several Regions they inhabit … Conquest over such people can give no just title.'[3]

Cook encountered Aboriginal people during his voyage. However, without their consent, on 22 August 1770, on Bedanug Island off the south-western tip of Cape York, he claimed possession of the eastern Australian coastline for King George III. Cook called this new territory New South Wales.

The British resolved to use their new territory of New South Wales as a convict settlement due to the growing number of people in their jails. These were full to overflowing as the agricultural revolution forced small farmers and poor labourers off the land and into the city where many engaged in crimes such as stealing for food. In 1786, Captain Arthur Phillip was appointed as the first governor and commander-in-chief of New South Wales.

Phillip travelled to New South Wales with the First Fleet, arriving in Botany Bay on 18 January 1788. He carried no instructions requiring him to seek the consent of Aboriginal people, only to 'open an intercourse with the natives, and to conciliate their affections, enjoining all our subjects to live in amity and kindness with them.'[4] On 26 January 1788, Phillip landed in Sydney Cove and planted the Union Jack, proclaiming New South Wales as a British colony. There was no ceding of sovereignty by the Aboriginal people. As described by the bipartisan Expert Panel that in 2012 reported on Indigenous constitutional recognition:

> It follows that ultimately the basis of settlement in Australia is and always has been the exertion of force by and on behalf of the British Crown. No-one asked permission to settle.

> No-one consented, no-one ceded. Sovereignty was not passed from the Aboriginal peoples by any actions of legal significance voluntarily taken by or on behalf of them.[5]

As the colony of New South Wales developed, the legal status of the continent's first peoples remained ambiguous. At best, the English governors were instructed to conciliate with and protect the Aboriginal 'natives' and maintain friendly relations.

The period of conciliation with Aboriginal people did not last long. From the earliest days, 'many convicts and marines stole from the Aborigines their fishing and hunting tackle, their women and sometimes their lives, just as the British government, in the person of Arthur Phillip, had already stolen their land'.[6] An inability to communicate also exacerbated cultural differences. The colonists 'failed to comprehend the reciprocal obligations set up by the Aborigines. They interpreted Aboriginal attempts to enforce those obligations – by helping themselves to British goods, and later, attacking those who refused to reciprocate – as casual pilfering and treacherous violence'.[7]

The views of the early settlers about Aboriginal people varied. There were competing theories of race and changing theories about racial equality during the late 18th and early 19th centuries. While racial equality found support in the Enlightenment and in Christianity and therefore influenced some of the early settlers, these ideas increasingly clashed with the economic aspirations of the arrivals and the resistance of Aboriginal populations to dispossession on the frontier. The deaths of Aboriginal people at the hands of British settlers and the Australian-born settlers associated with the economic and political development of Australia have become known as 'the

Killing Times' or 'Frontier Wars'. The first record of resistance by an Aboriginal group was in May 1788 around Sydney and the latest was the Coniston Massacre in 1928 in the Northern Territory.

These conflicts occurred because the settlers wanted to exploit the land for urban expansion and the development of the pastoral and other industries, and Aboriginal people were occupying those lands. The colonists continually required new land, which involved the settlers removing Aboriginal people from their country forcibly or through killing. As these conflicts took place, theories of racial hierarchy became increasingly popular. Settlers took comfort in the fiction that Aboriginal people were inferior, something that was supported by scientific and anthropological thinking from North America and Europe.

In 1803, the colony of Van Diemen's Land (later named Tasmania) was established and Lieutenant-Governor David Collins arrived with soldiers, convicts and free colonists with instructions to conciliate with the natives. Despite this, conflict began immediately as a result of the contest for land and resources. From 1813, exploration of inland Australia also continued and the colonists expanded rapidly, including into southern Queensland and central South Australia. Violence again ensued, much of it authorised by the state, as evidenced by Governor Lachlan Macquarie's Proclamation in 1816, which authorised reprisals against Aboriginal people. This demonstrates the way the law was used to validate massacres and also reflected the uncertain legal status of Aboriginal people: 'For the first fifty years the colonial legal system had trouble deciding whether the Aborigines should be treated as subjects of the Crown or foreign enemies who could be hunted down in reprisal raids and shot'.[8]

Towards Federation

The first convicts were sent to Sydney, and later to Van Diemen's Land, Port Macquarie, Moreton Bay and Norfolk Island. From the outset, convicts were the majority population of the British colony and thus the primary source of labour. Over time, free settlers also arrived and convicts began to work for them as well as the early landholders; indeed, a squatting movement saw settlers begin to expand throughout south-eastern Australia and the pastoral economy develop quickly. Squatting is an unlawful way of occupying land, but over time governments granted leases to many of these squatters.

As a consequence, the colonies began to expand across the continent. In 1823, the British Parliament separated the administration of Van Diemen's Land from New South Wales and granted both colonies a Legislative Council. Then, from 1825 to 1859, the remainder of the settlements emerged as the separate self-governing colonies of Western Australia, South Australia, Queensland and Victoria.

Over time, the grant of self-government to the Australian colonies fostered the idea that they could join together to form a new nation. This movement towards Federation was driven by a number of factors, including fear of common enemies, concern for immigration and inter-colonial trade and commerce, and an emerging sense of nationalism.

The Federation movement began in earnest with a speech

by Henry Parkes, the Premier of New South Wales. In 1889, at Tenterfield, he called for the colonies to 'unite and create a great national government for all Australia'.[9] He then wrote to the other colonial premiers proposing a meeting to discuss a constitution for the new nation, at which he famously remarked that the 'the crimson thread of kinship runs through us all'. By this he referred to common racial and British heritage of the colonists as the basis upon which the new nation might be founded.

Parkes initiated a decade of conventions and public debate, which culminated in a Constitution and the Australian Federation in 1901. The Constitution was drafted at two Constitutional Conventions. The main issues at the Conventions were the financial and trade issues arising from Federation, and how best to weigh the interests of the small states against those of the more populous states in the new federal Parliament. Customs duties, tariffs and the capacity of the upper house of the federal Parliament to veto money bills were of far greater concern to the Convention delegates than the rights of Aboriginal and Torres Strait Islander peoples. Indeed, no Indigenous person was present at either Convention, nor did any delegate seek to represent their interests.

Indigenous peoples had previously made demands for greater representation and involvement in colonial governance. From the 1840s, they petitioned the Crown against their brutal treatment by the British. For example, in 1846, Tasmanian Aboriginal people on Flinders Island petitioned Queen Victoria, and in 1881, Yorta Yorta men living on the Maloga Mission sent a petition to the Governor of New South Wales asking for land.

Led by William Barack, the people of Coranderrk, a reserve in south central Victoria, initiated several deputations to the colonial government in Melbourne. Petitions were also sent in the 1870s and 1880s, and in 1881 this led to the Parliamentary Coranderrk Inquiry. This was the only occasion in Victoria in the 19th century on which an official commission was called to examine Indigenous demands for land and self-determination.

Despite all of this, the process of drafting a constitution for the new nation continued without Indigenous input. The first Convention was held in Sydney in 1891 and was attended by representatives of the colonial parliaments. The draft constitution adopted by the 1891 Convention was to be put to a referendum in each colony, with a view to it being enacted for Australia by the United Kingdom Parliament. The proposal faltered when it lapsed in New South Wales without having gone to a referendum.

The process began afresh in 1895. The premiers of the colonies agreed to establish a popularly elected Convention to produce a further draft constitution to be put to the people in each colony at a referendum. This Convention met in Adelaide and Sydney in 1897, and in Melbourne in 1898. Popularly elected representatives were sent by New South Wales, South Australia, Tasmania and Victoria. Queensland was not represented at the Convention, and Western Australia sent parliamentary representatives rather than popularly elected delegates.

Rather than making a new start, the delegates to the 1897–98 Convention revised the draft constitution endorsed by the 1891 Convention. Under the leadership of Edmund Barton – later Australia's first prime minister and one of the first members of the High Court – the Convention refined the document to incorporate later compromises. This revised draft was put to the people of New South Wales, South Australia, Tasmania and Victoria. No referendum was held in Queensland or Western Australia. The draft constitution received majority support in each of the four colonies holding referendums, but was nevertheless deemed a failure in New South Wales because the number of people that voted for the draft did not reach the minimum of 80 000 required for success by the New South Wales Parliament.

The draft constitution was then amended at a conference in 1899 attended by the premiers of all six colonies. In 1899 and 1900 it was again put to the voters in the colonies, this time also in Queensland and Western Australia. On this occasion, the draft constitution was supported by a majority of voters in each colony. Large sections of the community were excluded from voting, including most women and many Aboriginal people. Women were able to vote for or against the draft constitution only in South Australia and Western Australia, while Aboriginal people were able to vote only in New South Wales, South Australia, Tasmania and Victoria. However, even where Aboriginal people had a legal entitlement to vote, there is no evidence that they were able to or encouraged to. Just as they were absent from every step in the drafting of Australia's Constitution, so too did they play no role in endorsing the document.

After the referendums of 1899 and 1900, a delegation representing the Australian colonies was sent to London to have the draft constitution enacted by the British Parliament. In the absence of a revolution or other severing of ties with Britain, the

Imperial Parliament still exercised ultimate authority over the Australian colonies. It was thus the source of power to which colonists turned to bring about the new Federation.

A Bill containing the draft constitution was introduced into the House of Commons. It completed its passage through the Imperial Parliament on 5 July 1900, was assented to by Queen Victoria on 9 July 1900 and came into force on 1 January 1901 as the *Commonwealth of Australia Constitution Act 1900*. Section 9 of the Act reads, 'The Constitution of the Commonwealth shall be as follows', and thereafter contains the entire text of the Australian Constitution.

The failure to include Aboriginal and Torres Strait Islander peoples in the move to Federation and the drafting of Australia's Constitution reflected how the colonists perceived them. There were a variety of positive anthropological and scientific opinions about Indigenous people, influenced by developments such as the end of slavery in 1833 throughout the British Empire and the 'upsurge of ... humanitarian sentiment in England'.[10] Despite this, a view took hold between 1850 and 1890 that Aboriginal people were a 'dying race', meaning that it was not expected that they would survive British settlement. This confounded the British Colonial Office, which was aware of the frontier massacres and maintained a desire to protect the Aborigines.

The dying race theory had a number of different meanings. It was primarily influenced by social Darwinism and the idea of 'survival of the fittest', but also had Christian connotations of doomed souls. Frontier killings and dispersals meant Aboriginal population numbers were dwindling, such that the dying race theory corresponded with local conditions. This was certainly influential in Tasmania where massacres had resulted in the near extinction of Aboriginal people. Such thinking was one reason why the framers of the Australian Constitution made no effort to include Aboriginal peoples in the new political settlement.

By the time of the 1890s Conventions, the race theories that provided a justification for the dispossession of Aboriginal peoples had taken hold more generally. Race-based thinking was also applied to other groups. Prior to Federation, many colonies had racially discriminatory employment laws. Maintaining these laws was a high priority and framers were driven by a desire to maintain race-based distinctions. For example, they rejected the idea of inserting certain human rights into the Constitution because of fears that this might protect, as citizens, 'Chinamen, Japanese, Hindoos, and other barbarians' in areas such as employment.[11]

The text of the Constitution

The Constitution brought about a system of government for the new Australian nation based upon notions of representative and responsible government. It also incorporated a separation of powers by which the courts could act as an independent check upon Parliament and government. The document also reflected the views and values of the framers about Aboriginal people and the people of other races.

The preamble to the British Act that brought about the Australian Constitution speaks of the values that underlie the document and the process leading to its creation. On the other hand, no mention is made of the long history of Aboriginal and Torres Strait Islander people on the Australian continent. That preamble states:

> WHEREAS the people of New South Wales, Victoria, South Australia, Queensland, and Tasmania, humbly relying on the blessing of Almighty God, have agreed to unite in one indissoluble Federal Commonwealth under the Crown of the United Kingdom of Great Britain and Ireland, and under the Constitution hereby established:
>
> And whereas it is expedient to provide for the admission into the Commonwealth of other Australasian Colonies and possessions of the Queen:
>
> Be it therefore enacted by the Queen's most Excellent Majesty, by and with the advice and consent of the Lords Spiritual and Temporal, and Commons, in this present Parliament assembled, and by the authority of the same, as follows ...[12]

These words do not mention the people of Western Australia because they only agreed to join the Federation after the preamble had been drafted.

The text of the 1901 Constitution made two references to Aboriginal people. Section 127 provided:

> In reckoning the numbers of the people of the Commonwealth, or of a State or other part of the Commonwealth, aboriginal natives shall not be counted.[13]

Section 127 was adopted to stop Western Australia and Queensland from using their large Aboriginal populations to gain extra seats in the federal Parliament and a higher share of federal tax revenue. This reflected the view that Aboriginal people should not be counted in determining representation and were not deserving of a share of government income. Expressing the fringe status of Aboriginal people of the time, Barton argued that it would 'not be considered fair to include the aborigines in population counts'.[14] The fact that Aboriginal people were excluded in this way without further debate at the Conventions reveals much about how they were viewed at the time.

This section operated in tandem with section 25 of the Constitution. Section 25 contemplated that the states would continue to prevent people of certain races from voting at their elections. It provided that, where this occurred, the races so excluded could not be counted in the population of that state that would be used to determine the state's representation in the federal Parliament.

Aboriginal people were also further marginalised in a new power granted to the Commonwealth Parliament. Section 51(xxvi), known as the 'races power', permitted the making of federal laws for:

> The people of any race, other than the aboriginal race in any State, for whom it is deemed necessary to make special laws.[15]

The exclusion of Aboriginal people from this power meant that laws for them were to be made instead by the states.

The races power was inserted into the Constitution to

enable the federal Parliament to pass laws that discriminate against the people of any race, other than the Aboriginal race. It was to allow the Commonwealth to pass the sort of laws already in existence prior to Federation aimed at 'the Indian, Afghan, and Syrian hawkers; the Chinese miners, laundrymen, market gardeners, and furniture manufacturers; the Japanese settlers and Kanaka plantation labourers of Queensland, and the various coloured races employed in the pearl fisheries of Queensland and Western Australia.'[16] In explaining the reasoning for this power, Sir Samuel Griffith, who later became the first Chief Justice of the High Court, observed:

> What I have had more particularly in my own mind was the immigration of coolies from British India, or any eastern people subject to civilised powers ... I maintain that no state should be allowed, because the federal parliament did not choose to make a law on the subject, to allow the state to be flooded by such people as I have referred to.[17]

Similarly, Barton suggested that such a power was needed to enable the Commonwealth to 'regulate the affairs of the people of coloured or inferior races who are in the Commonwealth.'[18] Summarising the effect of the power, John Quick and Robert Garran, the authors of the authoritative text on the Constitution at the time of its enactment, wrote:

> It enables the Parliament to deal with the people of any alien race after they have entered the Commonwealth; to localise them within defined areas, to restrict their migration, to confine them to certain occupations, or to give them special

> protection and secure their return after a certain period to the country whence they came.[19]

Some delegates spoke strongly against such a power. Josiah Symon, a former Attorney-General of South Australia, argued: 'It is monstrous to put a brand on these people when you admit them. It is degrading to us and our citizenship to do such a thing. If we say they are fit to be admitted amongst us, we ought not to degrade them by putting on them a brand of inferiority'.[20] However, lest it be thought that section 51(xxvi) might confer any protection from racial discrimination, Quick and Garran continued: 'On the contrary, it would seem that by sub-sec xxvi the federal Parliament will have power to pass special and discriminating laws relating to "the people of any race," and that such laws could not be challenged on the ground of unconstitutionality'.[21]

Despite the races power being the subject of extensive discussion, the Convention debates are silent as to why Aboriginal people were excluded from the section. Perhaps, to use the language of the time, it was the thought that the states, and not the Commonwealth, should 'smooth the dying pillow' of Aboriginal people.

Tasmanian Attorney-General Andrew Inglis Clark proposed that the new Constitution guarantee every citizen due process of law and the equal protection of the law. He based this upon the 14th amendment of the United States Constitution. This might have prevented the states from enacting and maintaining racially discriminatory laws.

The proposal for a due process clause was problematic in Australia because racially discriminatory laws excluding people from Asia and the Pacific from seeking a mining licence and working were seen as normal across the states. The early Australian colonies openly espoused racist sentiment that was reflected in their laws. The framers wanted to preserve such laws. The most outspoken on this was the premier of Western Australia, Sir John Forrest, who said: 'We have made a law that no Asiatic or African alien can get a miner's right or do any gold mining. Does the Convention wish to take [that] away from us ...?'[22] He went on:

> It is of no use for us to shut our eyes to the fact that there is a great feeling all over Australia against the introduction of coloured persons. It goes without saying that we do not like to talk about it, but still it is so. I do not want this clause to pass in a shape which would undo what is about to be done in most of the colonies, and what has already been done in Western Australia, in regard to that class of persons.[23]

Ultimately, a compromise was fashioned, with future High Court Justice Henry Higgins proposing a clause that became section 117 of the Constitution. Rather than protecting against racial discrimination or providing equality under the law, this provision says a person resident in one state cannot be 'subject in any other State to any disability or discrimination which would not be equally applicable to him if he were ... resident in such other State'. For example, a person residing in Queensland could not be denied a job in New South Wales because of their Queensland residency. The result was a very narrow form of protection. According to Higgins, this 'would allow Sir John Forrest ... to have his law with regard to Asiatics not being able to obtain miners' rights in Western Australia. There is no discrimination there based on residence or citizenship; it is simply based on colour and race'.[24]

The new Commonwealth Parliament

After the Constitution came into force, Australia's first general election was held on 29 and 30 March 1901. It led to a government being formed by Barton, and the first sitting of the new federal Parliament on 9 May. The importance of race-based distinctions became immediately apparent. One of the first pieces of legislation enacted by the new Parliament was the *Immigration Restriction Act 1901*, which prohibited the immigration into Australia of any person who, when asked by an officer, was unable to 'write out at dictation and sign in the presence of the officer a passage of fifty words in length in an European language directed by the officer'.[25] This was the means by which the White Australia policy was implemented.

Introducing the Bill, Prime Minister Barton argued:

> I do not think either that the doctrine of the equality of man was really ever intended to include racial equality. There is no racial equality. There is that basic inequality. These races are, in comparison with white races – I think no one wants convincing of this fact – unequal and inferior. The doctrine of the equality of man was never intended to apply to the equality of the Englishman and the Chinaman. There is deep-set difference, and we see no prospect and no promise of its ever being effaced. Nothing in this world can

> put these two races upon an equality. Nothing we can do by cultivation, by refinement, or by anything else will make some races equal to others.[26]

On Aboriginal people, Alfred Deakin, Australia's first federal Attorney-General and second Prime Minister, said:

> Little more than a hundred years ago Australia was a Dark Continent in every sense of the term. There was not a white man within its borders. In another century the probability is that Australia will be a White Continent with not a black or even dark skin amongst its inhabitants. The aboriginal race has died out in the South and is dying fast in the North and West even where most gently treated. Other races are to be excluded by legislation if they are tinted to any degree.[27]

Soon after, Parliament passed a law setting out who could vote in federal elections. The *Commonwealth Franchise Act 1902* was progressive for its time in extending the franchise to women. It had also been proposed that the franchise encompass Aboriginal people, but this was strongly resisted and ultimately defeated. Among its opponents were Isaac Isaacs, later a judge of the High Court and Australia's first native-born Governor-General, who suggested that Aboriginal people 'have not the intelligence, interest, or capacity' to vote.[28] Similarly, Higgins thought it 'utterly inappropriate ... [to] ask them to exercise an intelligent vote'.[29]

As finally enacted, the law denied federal voting rights to every 'aboriginal native of Australia ... unless so entitled under section forty-one of the Constitution'.[30] Section 41 says that a person is guaranteed the vote in federal elections if they can vote for the more numerous House of their state Parliament. However, where Aboriginal people were entitled to vote in a state, such as South Australia, a vote in federal elections was in practice still denied to them. The ban on Aboriginal people voting in federal elections continued until 1962. Even then, full equality at federal elections did not occur until 1983, when the law was amended to make enrolment for and voting in federal elections compulsory for Indigenous people, as it had been for decades for other Australians.

A growing mood for change

Today, when the High Court interprets the Constitution, it turns to the records of the Convention debates during the 1890s to understand the intention of the drafters. Yet there is no record of Aboriginal and Torres Strait Islander people playing any role in the drafting of the Constitution or the process that led to the creation of the Australian nation. Nor did they take part in the delegation that travelled to Britain to have that document enacted. Nor is there any record of Indigenous people being consulted about this, or their consent being sought to bring about a new nation on their ancestral lands. Instead, the Constitution was drafted to exclude Aboriginal people, who many of the colonists viewed as a 'dying race'.

Over time, frontier violence gave way to a new situation for Aboriginal people in Australia. Excluded from the political settlement that brought about the new nation, Aboriginal people found themselves forced onto missions and reserves. The

Constitution meant that responsibility for their welfare fell to the states, which initiated what is known as the Protection Era.

The word 'protection' is used because this period ushers in a system of segregation on the basis of race. Aboriginal people were herded off country, often at gunpoint, and placed onto designated parcels of land often surrounded by wire to separate them from mainstream society. The Protection Era is distinguished by special, seemingly benevolent legislation aimed at protecting Aboriginal people from the 'worst effects of contact with Europeans,' including diseases and violence.[31] However, these laws were draconian. They forced Aboriginal people off country to live on state- and missionary-run reserves. Every aspect of their lives was regulated, from marriage, employment and freedom of movement, to regulation of their work and how pay from that work was to be spent. The era was characterised by overtly discriminatory laws in which Aboriginal people were denied equality in almost every aspect of their lives.

One of the worst features of the Protection Era was the removal of children from their families – known as the Stolen Generations. This was often justified by invoking the 'protection' of Aboriginal and Torres Strait Islander people, but the forcible removal of children was intended to weaken Aboriginal culture and kinship and to debilitate many manifestations of culture such as language and ceremony. It also led to social and medical issues arising as a consequence of removal. However, this treatment did not go unnoticed. A growing sense of injustice arising from the treatment of Aboriginal and Torres Strait Islander peoples led many Australians to argue for change, including to the Constitution.

2

THE 1967 REFERENDUM

On 27 May 1967, Australians voted Yes to change the Constitution. They did so in overwhelming numbers never seen in Australia – and not seen since. Exactly what this referendum achieved has long been the subject of debate and misunderstanding. Indeed, the vote has attained somewhat of a mythical status that far exceeds the legal changes it brought about. Even to this day, it is said that the referendum meant that Aboriginal people became Australian citizens, or that they got the vote. The referendum achieved neither of these things.

The changes to the Constitution brought about by the referendum were modest, and had more to do with altering Australia's federal architecture than creating new rights for Aboriginal and Torres Strait Islander peoples. The referendum deleted two sets of words from the Constitution. First, it removed an exclusion from the races power in section 51(xxvi) that had prevented the federal Parliament from enacting laws for Aboriginal people. Second, it repealed section 127, which had prevented Aboriginal people from being included in 'reckoning the numbers of the people of the Commonwealth'.

Both of these provisions referred to Aboriginal people in negative ways, either by way of removing them as a subject of federal power, or by excluding them from the count of the people of the Commonwealth used for determining representation in the federal Parliament. The deletions did not, however, grant

Aboriginal people any new rights or recognition. In terms of recognition, the referendum removed the only references to Aboriginal peoples in the document, leaving nothing in their place. The referendum also extended the races power to them without indicating that the power should only be used for their benefit. This opened up the possibility that the power might be used to discriminate against them.

Modern recollections of the 1967 referendum also overlook the fact that Australians voted that day on another proposal to change the Constitution. A second, unsuccessful, idea was put to the people that would have removed the requirement in the Constitution that the House of Representatives have twice as many members as the Senate. It was this second proposal, seeking to break the link, or 'nexus' as it was called, between the houses of Parliament, that attracted the lion's share of public debate. This proposal, rather than the referendum on Indigenous peoples, was the main focus for most of Australia's political leaders, including the government of the day.

Decades of debate

The 1967 referendum was the product of decades of agitation and advocacy by Aboriginal and Torres Strait Islander peoples and their supporters. The idea that the Commonwealth should have power over Aboriginal peoples can be traced back to shortly after Federation, when the idea was suggested as a means of responding to the 'problem' of Aboriginal people being a 'dying race'. For example, in 1913, a committee on Aboriginal welfare, established by the Australasian Association for the

Advancement of Science, argued that 'the Aboriginal problem will only be solved when all that is left of the race is made a single and National responsibility and cared for in a National way'. The committee argued that this could create a 'national sentiment of sympathy and pity … towards this unfortunate race whom we have dispossessed'.[1]

Similarly, in the late 1920s, the Association for the Protection of the Native Races of Australasia and Polynesia argued that the federal and not the state tier of government should have responsibility for passing laws for Aboriginal peoples:

> The method of relying upon State and Colonial Governments has been tried from the earliest days of colonisation, and has undeniably failed … It is a recognised political principle that the wider the area from which the governing power is derived, the larger the task set, the wider and more statesmanlike the policy is likely to be. It follows as a corollary that the Federal government is likely to deal with the whole problem more adequately than the State Governments.[2]

The dissenting report to the 1929 Royal Commission on the Constitution agreed, and recommended that the Commonwealth should have responsibility for Indigenous peoples.

Meanwhile, Indigenous peoples were engaged in advocacy for their rights and self-determination. The Australian Aboriginal Progressive Association (AAPA) was formed in Sydney in 1924. It called for an Aboriginal board to sit below the Commonwealth government, and for Indigenous self-determination. In 1927, the AAPA launched a manifesto that sought: 'The control of Aboriginal affairs, apart from common law rights shall be vested in a board of management comprised of capable educated Aboriginals under a chairman to be appointed by the government'.

In 1933, Joe Anderson – also known as King Burraga – from the Salt Pan Creek on the Georges River, New South Wales, called for representation in the federal Parliament, and a corroboree for all Aboriginal people in New South Wales to organise a petition to the King. Four years later, in 1937, William Cooper, a Yorta Yorta man and inaugural Secretary of the Australian Aborigines League, organised a petition to the King, demanding Aboriginal representation in Parliament. Cooper had spent several years gathering a large number of signatures on the petition, from all around the country. The Australian government acknowledged receipt of the petition, but refused to forward it to the King.

A few months later, in January 1938, the Australian Aborigines' League, together with the Aborigines Progressive Association, initiated a 'Day of Mourning', calling for Commonwealth control of Indigenous affairs and a national policy. Speakers included renowned Aboriginal leaders and activists: Jack Patten, who was the first president of the Aborigines Progressive Association; William Ferguson, a Wiradjuri man who founded the Aborigines Progressive Association; Doug Nicholls, a Yorta Yorta man; and Pearl Gibbs, a Ngemba or Muruwari woman and a member of the Aborigines Progressive Association. The organisers of the Day of Mourning also arranged the first ever Indigenous deputation to the Prime Minister. They presented him with a Ten-Point Plan for Indigenous equality. Fundamental to this was citizenship rights. The demand was phrased as:

> WE, representing THE ABORIGINES OF AUSTRALIA, assembled in conference at the Australian Hall, Sydney, on the 26th day of January, 1938, this being the 150th Anniversary of the Whiteman's seizure of our country, HEREBY MAKE PROTEST against the callous treatment of our people by the whitemen during the past 150 years, AND WE APPEAL to the Australian nation of today to make new laws for the education and care of Aborigines, we ask for a new policy which will raise our people TO FULL CITIZEN STATUS and EQUALITY WITHIN THE COMMUNITY.[3]

However, the Constitution remained a barrier, as it precluded the Commonwealth from legislating about Indigenous peoples.

In 1944, the Curtin government unsuccessfully sought power over Indigenous peoples in the failed Post-War Reconstruction and Democratic Rights referendum. This proved only to be a temporary setback, with the debate stepping up a notch in the late 1940s and 1950s, including through the advocacy of Aboriginal organisations such as the Aborigines Progressive Association and the Australian Aborigines' League. This reflected developments not only in Australia, but internationally, such as the Universal Declaration of Human Rights, which in 1948 recognised 'the inherent dignity' and 'the equal and inalienable rights of all members of the human family'.[4]

In 1949, Indigenous returned servicemen were given the right to vote. In 1950, the House of Representatives unanimously moved a motion that the Commonwealth:

a Exercises national responsibility for Aboriginal people and cooperates with the States.

b Works towards the social advancement as well as the protection of Aborigines.
c Provides additional finance and effective administration.[5]

This was accompanied by a growing sense that Aboriginal people should have the same rights as other Australians. For example, in 1957, opposition leader HV Evatt declared in Parliament: 'the only thing to be done with the Australian Aboriginal, full-blood or otherwise, is to give him the benefit of the same laws as apply to every other Australian'.[6]

In 1962, the vote in federal elections was extended to all Indigenous Australians, which strengthened the case for constitutional reform. It was clearly absurd for Indigenous Australians to have the vote, only for section 127 of the Constitution to deny them the right to be counted for the purposes of determining electoral districts.

Advocacy for change waxed and waned, but was finally put on the political agenda by the efforts of many people, including civil rights campaigners Lady Jessie Street and Faith Bandler. A campaign was built around the notion that Aboriginal people should have full rights as citizens and that their welfare should be a federal responsibility. In 1958, this led to the creation of the Federal Council for Aboriginal Advancement (renamed in 1964 as the Federal Council for the Advancement of Aborigines and Torres Strait Islanders).

Over the following decade, this organisation became the leading proponent for constitutional change and for the Yes case at the 1967 referendum. The first and primary principle of the body was that Aboriginal people should be granted 'equal citizenship with other Australian citizens'.[7] It sought this by way of repealing any federal or state legislation that discriminated against Aboriginal people and amending the Australian Constitution to give the federal Parliament the power to legislate for them. The body advocated for these changes through community and political activism, including public events, speaking tours and petitions presented to Parliament.

The movement for constitutional reform continued to make strides through the early 1960s, including through the Freedom Ride in 1965 in which 30 University of Sydney students, including Aboriginal activist Charles Perkins and future New South Wales Supreme Court chief justice Jim Spigelman, travelled through rural New South Wales to draw attention to discrimination against Indigenous people. That same year, Western Australia and Queensland became the last states to grant Aboriginal people the right to vote. By 1967 there was consensus on the need for reform, both in the community and across political parties.

Despite many years of advocacy, the change to the Constitution only achieved solid political backing in the final days of the Menzies government. Prime Minister Robert Menzies had been reluctant to attempt any constitutional reform since his failure to convince the Australian people to ban the Communist Party of Australia at the 1951 referendum. Nevertheless, in 1965, his government committed to putting two questions to the people, one concerning Aboriginal peoples, and the other seeking to break the nexus between the sizes of the two Houses of federal Parliament.

Even then, there was no rush for these questions to be taken to the ballot box, and in the meantime Menzies was succeeded as Prime Minister on Australia Day 1966 by his Treasurer, Harold Holt. Holt also took his time, and showed no special interest in the proposals. However, after winning the November 1966 general election, he needed to keep the Liberal Party's public commitment to put both questions to the people, and so a referendum was finally put on 27 May 1967.

The proposals put to the people

The proposal on Aboriginal peoples at the 1967 referendum included two components. Both reflected fundamental changes in Australia's idea of Aboriginal people since Federation. Neither of the 1890s Conventions that debated the Constitution had made serious mention of Indigenous people. Cast as a 'dying race', they played no meaningful role in its drafting. While the preamble to the Constitution suggests that 'the people ... have agreed to unite', it makes no mention of Aboriginal people or their occupation of the lands upon which the new nation was formed.

The operative provisions of the Constitution were also based upon the exclusion of Indigenous peoples, and even discrimination against them. As drafted in 1901, the Constitution made two references to Aboriginal people. The races power in section 51(xxvi) empowered the federal Parliament to make laws with respect to: 'The people of any race, *other than the aboriginal race in any State*, for whom it is deemed necessary to make special laws'. The words in italics meant that the power could not be used by the federal Parliament to make laws for Aboriginal peoples, as this was to be a state and not a federal responsibility. The 1967 referendum deleted the words in italics, thereby granting legislative power over Aboriginal people to the federal Parliament. The referendum did not deny the states the continuing ability to legislate for Aboriginal peoples. It simply meant that both tiers of government now had the power to do so.

The referendum also repealed section 127, which had provided: 'In reckoning the numbers of the people of the Commonwealth, or of a state or other part of the Commonwealth, aboriginal natives shall not be counted'. The section meant that Aboriginal people were not to be counted for the purpose of determining the size and distribution of electorates for the federal Parliament. Even though the section arguably only applied for electoral purposes, it had a wider impact on how Aboriginal people were counted in the national census. The Expert Panel that in 2012 reported on the constitutional recognition of Indigenous peoples described the situation in this way:

> At the first Australian census in 1911, only those 'aboriginal natives' living near white settlements were counted, and the main population tables included only those of half or less Aboriginal descent. Details of 'half-caste' (but not 'full-blood') Aboriginal people were included in the tables on race. Details of 'full-blood' Aboriginal people were included in separate tables. The practice was followed in all censuses up until 1966.[8]

This practice reflected the opinion of the Commonwealth Attorney-General at the time of the 1911 census that section 127 meant that censuses and other government publications of population figures could not include those who were referred to as 'full-blooded Aborigines'.[9]

In electoral terms, the effect of section 127 was a substantial under-weighting of the Aboriginal and Torres Strait Islander vote. This reflected the view widely held at Federation that they were not entitled to take part in Australia's democratic processes. Well before 1967, national attitudes had changed. The ban on Aboriginal people voting in federal elections was removed in 1962. A sense had also emerged that it was no longer acceptable to have a provision in the Constitution such as section 127, which was so obviously discriminatory. Rooting out this constitutionalised discrimination was an important part of changing Australia's conception of itself as a nation.

Attitudes had also changed by this time on whether the Commonwealth should be able to make laws for Indigenous peoples. By 1967, the states were moving towards uniformity in Indigenous policy, but gaps remained. Why, it was asked, should an Indigenous person have freedom of movement in New South Wales, but upon crossing the Queensland border need permission to enter a hotel? Why did only South Australia apply internationally recognised labour standards to Indigenous employees? Above all, one issue predominated: when it came to Aboriginal disadvantage, why should the Commonwealth have all the money, but none of the responsibility?

Support for the referendum came from all quarters. Every major party and many community figures supported the change. Letters to newspapers ran almost unequivocally in favour of a Yes vote. The unique national consensus was reflected in the absence of a No campaign. Even the 'for and against' booklet sent to voters to inform them of the referendum only contained arguments for change. This was because federal law required the 'against' case in the booklet to be written by the parliamentarians who had voted against the change, and on this occasion not one parliamentarian had done so.

Where there was opposition, it lay at the margins of the debate. Some argued a losing battle for state power, saying that power should remain with the states so they could fashion locally appropriate laws. Others took the opposite tack, arguing that the Commonwealth should have no power to make race-based laws at all, for that was the first step towards segregation and apartheid. Neither of these arguments had an impact. The Australian people had made up their minds to move on from the past and were swept up in the notion that voting Yes would remedy past injustices and forge a brighter path forward.

Public discussion of the referendum tended not to mention the changes to the text of the Constitution. The focus was instead on the symbolic nature of the shift. The media mostly covered the issue only in broad and positive terms. For *The Age*, for example, the question was a 'simple matter of humanity ... [and] a test of Australia's standing in the world'.[10] It said the question posed to Australians was whether they would yet recognise that 'Aborigines [should] be regarded as completely human'.[11] Other newspapers took a similar approach, with the *Sydney Morning Herald* running a front-page photo of two children, one Aboriginal and one white, gazing happily at each other as they walked down a laneway hand in hand.

The media coverage reflected the campaign run by the Yes case, both before the referendum campaign and during it. The change was portrayed in general terms as being 'Towards Equal

Citizenship for Aborigines', despite the fact that, as a matter of law, Aboriginal people were included as citizens when the concept of Australian citizenship was first created by the *Nationality and Citizenship Act 1948*.

Nonetheless, the idea of attaining citizenship rights was a major part of the campaign, with leaders such as Faith Bandler arguing that the change would grant Aboriginal people 'full citizenship rights and nothing less'. Others used the same theme, but in more general terms, with Aboriginal leader Chicka Dixon arguing for a Yes vote because 'I want to be accepted by white Australians as a person' and because he wanted to see 'white Australians finally, after 179 years, affirming at last that they believe we are human beings'.[12] Similarly, the Federal Council for Aboriginal Advancement urged the media to encourage a Yes vote to 'Aboriginal rights' and 'to give the Aborigines full citizenship rights'.[13] One advertisement run by the Council simply exhorted 'Right Wrongs Write YES for Aborigines!' accompanied by a picture of an Aboriginal baby.

Constructing the debate in this way proved highly effective in building a compelling and emotive case for change. However, it also fuelled misconceptions around the referendum. It is no surprise, given the rhetoric used at the time and the fact that many Australians know little about their Constitution, that many people still believe today the referendum dealt with fundamental questions of justice and Aboriginal rights, such as their status as citizens and ability to vote. These misconceptions have sometimes been accompanied by the myth that the referendum overrode a Flora and Fauna Act by which Aboriginal people were treated as part of Australia's native wildlife. In fact, no such Act has ever existed.

Exaggerated ideas about the changes brought about by the 1967 referendum are a problem. They undermine understandings of our legal and democratic system, and place a barrier in the way of future constitutional change.

If the 1967 referendum had already achieved the grand ideals expressed at the time, why is it necessary to hold a second referendum on the same topic? Part of the task, then, of convincing Australians to vote Yes at any contemporary referendum on constitutional recognition of Aboriginal peoples, is to first explain the limited nature of what was brought about in 1967. It is only once the modest legal scope of that referendum is understood, including the fact that it removed all references to Aboriginal people without inserting anything positive in their place, that it becomes clear that the referendum left behind unfinished business still worthy of debate today.

This unfinished business includes the fact that the referendum did not alter provisions enabling race-based discrimination. The races power itself is the prime example of this. The scope of the power was extended to Aboriginal people in 1967 without altering the fact that the section was drafted to enable discrimination against people on the basis of their race. As a result, the referendum opened the door for the power to be used to make laws beneficial or adverse to Aboriginal people. The negative possibility did not get much public attention at the time, overwhelmed as everyone was by the positive messages surrounding the referendum, including as to how an expanded races power could be used to enact national laws for the welfare of Aboriginal peoples. This gave rise, in the words of former Chief Justice of the High Court Robert French, to a 'tension ... between these beneficial objectives and the predominantly negative discrimination envisaged by the drafters of the original provision.'[14]

Nevertheless, some people did explain at the time that the referendum could have unintended and unfortunate consequences for Aboriginal peoples. One of Australia's leading constitutional lawyers, Geoffrey Sawer, warned that 'the dubious origins of the [races power], and the dangerous potentialities of adverse discriminatory treatment which it contains' meant that 'the complete repeal of the section would be preferable to any amendment intended to extend its possible benefits to the Aborigines.'[15] Similarly, Federal Liberal parliamentarian William (Billy) Wentworth, a prominent supporter of reform and subsequently Australia's first federal Minister for Aboriginal Affairs, wrote in the *Sydney Morning Herald* in 1965 that extending the races power to Aboriginal people in this way could be a 'cure ... worse than the disease ... [as] to remove these words would subject Aborigines to potential discrimination rather than protect them from it.'[16]

Wentworth argued, instead, for replacing the entire text of the races power with a new power to make laws for 'the advancement of the Aboriginal natives of the Commonwealth of Australia', along with a new section 117A to prohibit the Commonwealth and the states from maintaining any law 'which subjects any person who has been born or naturalised with the Commonwealth of Australia to any discrimination or disability within the Commonwealth by reason of his racial origin'. In 1966, Wentworth introduced a private members Bill into Parliament to bring about these changes, but it was not passed, and the government instead proceeded with its more limited proposal.

The 1967 referendum also failed to make any change to section 25 of the Constitution, which is headed 'Provision as to races disqualified from voting'. It provides that, for the purpose of determining how many members each state shall have in the House of Representatives, 'if by the law of any State all persons of any race are disqualified from voting at elections for the more numerous House of the Parliament of the State, then, in reckoning the number of the people of the State or of the Commonwealth, persons of that race resident in that State shall not be counted'. Section 25 lowers the population count of a state if that state disqualifies people of a particular race from voting, and thus penalises it by restricting its parliamentary representation. However, in doing so, the provision acknowledges that Aboriginal and other racial groups can be so disqualified.

Attempts have been made to repeal section 25, but without success. One attempt was made at the 1967 referendum, but not as part of the proposal dealing with the races power and section 127. The proposed repeal was actually included in a second question put on the same day. The focus of that question was not section 25, but rather the idea that voters should break the 'nexus' between the sizes of the House of Representatives and the Senate. In the Constitution, the framers set out in section 24 that the House must be, as near as practicable, twice the size of the Senate. For most of Australia's history to that point, there had been 36 Senators (six from each state) and approximately 72 members of the lower house.

In 1949, the Chifley Labor government increased the size of both Houses. The Senate was increased from 36 to 60 members and the House from 74 to 121. Despite this increase, rapid population growth meant that Australians were represented by far fewer Commonwealth parliamentarians per head of population than had been the case at Federation. In 1901, there was about one member of Parliament for every 50 000 Australians; by 1967, that number was 94 000.

Both major parties were reluctant to increase the size of the House because that would require a proportionate increase in the size of the Senate. Because of the Senate's system of proportional voting, the effect would be to increase the power of minor parties and possibly independents. These facts had formed the basis of a recommendation in the 1959 report of the bipartisan Joint Committee on Constitutional Review of the federal Parliament to break the nexus between the sizes of the Houses. In addition to repealing section 25, the nexus proposal sought to do three things: it would remove any link between the size of the Houses of Commonwealth Parliament; it would set a maximum number of Members of the House, being no more than one for every 85 000 Australians; and it would set a minimum number of Senators, being ten per state. The key to the proposal from the government's perspective was the first of these, the breaking of the nexus. The other two parts to the proposal were designed, ultimately unsuccessfully, to alleviate concerns that the proposal was an attack on the Senate.

For its proponents, an increase in the size of Parliament was necessary for effective representative government. The parliamentarian-to-voter ratio was said to be too low for representatives to properly respond to their constituents' needs. Not only were parliamentarians representing many more people than in the past, they were saddled with far greater responsibilities as the Commonwealth had entered into fields that had traditionally been the responsibility of the states. If there were an increase in the size of the House so that constituents could be effectively represented, proponents argued, the question is whether that should necessarily flow on to an increase in the size of the Senate. Should an increase on one side of the equation necessarily cause an increase on the other? For the advocates of change, the answer was No. This was the case that Harold Holt and the leaders of the Country Party (John McEwen) and Labor Opposition (Gough Whitlam) took to the people. They had the support of all 124 members of the House and 50 of the 60 members of the Senate.

Against the heavy artillery of the major parties was a motley crew of ten Senators. Most prominent were Vincent Gair, federal leader of the Democratic Labor Party (DLP), Frank McManus, Victorian DLP representative, and Reginald Wright, Tasmanian Liberal representative. They were supported by three other Liberal Senators, two Country Party Senators and two Independents. The No campaign mobilised quickly and rallied under the simple banner of 'no more politicians'. The claim was this: the only check on the size of the House is that a government wanting to expand the House must also expand the Senate. If you take away that check, they said, greed will lead to ever more politicians in Canberra. The No campaign was vigorous and effective.

Even as the press stepped up its coverage, Australians continued to suffer widespread ignorance and confusion about the proposal. Australians did not understand the word 'nexus'; nor did they understand the constitutional principle that the proposal was targeted at – the tying together of the sizes of the Senate and House. As referendum day approached, Holt targeted the No campaign. He called opponents 'childish' and spouters of prejudice and ignorance.[17] When Holt spoke on the referendum, his focus remained on the question of the nexus. Just a fifth of his key speech delivered on the night of 15 May – about two minutes – was devoted to what was known as the 'Aboriginals proposal'. The press reported that, by and large, the Aboriginals question was ignored by the parties.

Outcomes of the referendum

On referendum day, Australians voted in very different ways for the nexus and Aboriginals proposals. Only the latter succeeded in gaining the required national majority of Yes votes and a majority of Yes votes in a majority of the six states. The results, along with the questions actually put to voters, appear overleaf.[18]

As these results demonstrate, the Aboriginals proposal streaked ahead. Indeed, it recorded the highest national Yes vote for any referendum proposal ever put to the people. The change was supported overwhelmingly in every state, and nationally more than nine in ten formal votes were Yes votes. The lowest Yes vote was in Western Australia, but still more than eight in ten Western Australians supported the proposal, thereby making it the most successful referendum ever in that state. The largest No vote of any area was recorded in the Western Australian rural district of Kalgoorlie, where 8888 voters – or 29 per cent – were against the change.

The pattern Australia-wide for the Aboriginals proposal was for extremely strong Yes votes in the cities and slightly lower

Yes votes in rural and regional areas. The differences in attitude between electors in regional areas, where there was a higher concentration of Indigenous people, and those in urban areas disturbed many. The referendum's success was unquestioned, but the attitudes it revealed were disappointing to some. Who, it was asked, would vote against a proposal to count Indigenous Australians in determining electoral boundaries and to give the Commonwealth power to make laws for their welfare?

Most Australians voted the opposite way for the nexus proposal. At the final count, barely four in ten Australians supported a proposal that had the approval of the three major parties, the bipartisan Joint Committee on Constitutional Review and much of the press. Only New South Wales returned a Yes vote, in its case one of 51.0 per cent. The results in the other states were disastrous for proponents. Victoria, Holt's home state, recorded a Yes vote of barely more than 30 per cent, which remains the lowest Yes vote ever recorded by that state. Tasmanians said No in a greater proportion than any other state, with close to eight in ten (76.9 per cent) voting against the reform.

The day after the referendum, Holt left to travel overseas. Rather than focusing on the extraordinary moment of national consensus recorded in the vote on the Aboriginals proposal, he focused on the failure of the nexus proposal. Rather than labelling 27 May as a victory for Aboriginal Australians, he labelled the referendum a 'victory for prejudice and misrepresentation.'[19] Holt blamed Australians: 'the majority of electors chose to ignore the advice of those to whom they normally look for guidance.'[20] The nexus proposal was also

Question 1

Do you approve the proposed law for the alteration of the Constitution entitled 'An Act to alter the Constitution so that the number of Members of the House of Representatives may be increased without necessarily increasing the number of Senators'?

State	For	%	Against	%	Informal
New South Wales	1 087 694	51.01	1 044 458	48.99	34 355
Victoria	496 826	30.87	1 112 506	69.13	21 262
Queensland	370 200	44.13	468 673	55.87	9855
South Australia	186 344	33.91	363 120	66.09	11 380
Western Australia	114 841	29.05	280 523	70.95	10 302
Tasmania	42 764	23.06	142 660	76.94	3821
National Total	2 298 669	40.25	3 411 940	59.75	90 975

Not Carried

Question 2

Do you approve the proposed law for the alteration of the Constitution entitled 'An Act to alter the Constitution so as to omit certain words relating to the people of the Aboriginal race in any state so that Aboriginals are to be counted in reckoning the population'?

State	For	%	Against	%	Informal
New South Wales	1 949 036	91.46	182 010	8.54	35 461
Victoria	1 525 026	94.68	85 611	5.32	19 957
Queensland	748 612	89.21	90 587	10.79	9529
South Australia	473 440	86.26	75 383	13.74	12 021
Western Australia	319 823	80.95	75 282	19.05	10 561
Tasmania	167 176	90.21	18 134	9.79	3935
National Total	5 183 113	90.77	527 007	9.23	91 464

Carried

the main focus for the press. Page one of the *Sunday Herald* on 28 May recorded the Yes vote on Aboriginals in small type, before blaring in big, bold capitals: 'AUSTRALIA SAYS NO ON NEXUS.'[21]

The press had its eye on the political ramifications of the No vote for the nexus proposal, but the community campaigners who had fought the Aboriginals proposal saw things differently. Cast as a referendum that would recognise Aboriginal rights and even their inherent humanity, it is no surprise that its supporters saw the outcome as a landmark in Australian history and as a defining social and political event. In this respect, the response exceeded the narrow confines of the legal changes actually brought about. Hence, Bandler has said of the result that 'we went mad with excitement,'[22] while Jackie Huggins, a Bidjara/Pitjara and Biri Birri Gubba Juru woman, remembers as a young girl 'the shrieks of joy after the result was announced, laughter and a mass of tears.'[23]

Others have spoken of how it immediately changed the way Aboriginal people saw themselves within the community. In the aftermath of the referendum: 'There were black people on the streets in a way we have never seen them ... People were up, had washed their children, combed their hair and got themselves up in their very best gear and walked out in the streets of Brisbane, down Queen Street where they never went.'[24] Similarly, even though Aboriginal people were legally entitled to vote in federal elections before the 1967 referendum, it was only after the referendum that many felt able and willing to exercise that right. Although the vote did not establish Aboriginal peoples as Australian citizens, as they already possessed that status, it did mean that many saw themselves in this way for the first time, and were treated by more members of the community as possessing such rights.

It is only over time that Australians have come to see the true significance of the 1967 referendum. By the time of the 40th anniversary of the referendum in 2007, the reaction to the two polls was reversed. The focus was firmly on the Yes vote cast by Australians to remove discrimination against Aboriginal peoples and enable laws to be made on their behalf. Little or no attention was paid to the nexus proposal, with many Australians not even realising that on referendum day in 1967 two votes had been cast.

It is clear with the benefit of hindsight that, beyond the legal changes brought about by the referendum, it was a watershed moment in Australia's political and social affairs. It emboldened Indigenous groups and reinforced their public advocacy. Many took strength from the overwhelming success of the poll. The unprecedented Yes vote was also interpreted as a strong mandate for the making of national laws and policy on Indigenous affairs.

Nothing, however, in the changes to the Constitution required the Commonwealth to take over authority for Aboriginal affairs. It merely gave the federal Parliament a power, like that already held by the states, to make laws in this area if it so wished. Indeed, the view of the Holt government soon after the referendum was that it had no intention of taking over responsibility in the area. Bandler commented that the government had made 'a mockery of the referendum ... It is as if the electorate had never made any moral commitment to do a great deal more for Aborigines.'[25] Bandler here touched upon the political power of the referendum. The momentum created by an overwhelming vote of the Australian people in favour of Aboriginal rights and better treatment for Aboriginal peoples could not be ignored. Federal inaction was no longer possible.

This potential of the referendum was not realised until the election of the Whitlam government in 1972. It interpreted the referendum not only as providing legal power to the Commonwealth in the field, but a political mandate to do so. This led the Whitlam and subsequent governments to exert federal authority through wide-ranging legislation in areas such as land rights, cultural heritage and ultimately native title, and also through government programs designed to overcome Indigenous disadvantage. Many of these laws and programs could have been undertaken by the Commonwealth with the powers it already had prior to the 1967 referendum, but the referendum provided the catalyst for change. It is in this sense, more than in the legal changes actually brought about, that the 1967 referendum was a turning point for Aboriginal and Torres Strait Islander peoples and their relationship with government.

3

A NEW ERA?

The success of the 1967 referendum sparked a flurry of activity in Aboriginal and Torres Strait Islander communities. Buoyed by the result, they sought to advance a more concrete agenda by way of new federal legislation to enable their aspirations such as land rights. This reflected an expectation that the federal Parliament would immediately use the expanded races power to fulfil the aspirations of Indigenous peoples. The reality was very different.

Initially, the federal Parliament was slow to use its new power. Though, over the years, it legislated for a limited range of institutions, rights and protections, Indigenous hopes faded that the referendum result would lead to reforms such as the negotiation of a treaty. In time, a different concern emerged, that the races power might actually be used to discriminate against Aboriginal people, something that few foresaw when they voted Yes in 1967. By the turn of the new century, this fear became enmeshed with a new journey initiated by Aboriginal and Torres Strait Islander peoples to seek reform of the Constitution to repair the defects of 1967 and to build a stronger foundation for working with government and the broader Australian community.

After the 1967 referendum

There was much anticipation among campaigners, such as Faith Bandler, that the 1967 referendum would herald a new era of law and policy making in Aboriginal affairs. Bandler said the victory 'now gave the federal government a constituted right to create laws that would support the endeavours of Aborigines or Islanders'.[1]

In the aftermath of the poll, incremental developments occurred at a federal level under the Holt and McMahon governments, including the appointment of William Wentworth as Australia's first Minister for Aboriginal Affairs. However, many people were frustrated by the cautious approach taken by the Commonwealth to its new power. This reflected an ongoing deference to the states. Many Aboriginal and Torres Strait Islander peoples noticed that, despite the referendum, 'discrimination did not end overnight' in their lives.[2]

Nevertheless, the referendum animated much political activity in the community. It gave new life to Aboriginal activism as people continued to struggle for land rights and self-determination with renewed vigour. Some of this was not a result of the referendum, but had its genesis in the earliest forms of resistance, including the political movement for sovereignty that 'had begun at the time a colony was first established in Sydney [and] shared a heart with freedom fighters like Pemulwuy'.[3]

Many people were motivated by the Gurindji in the Northern Territory. In 1966, led by Vincent Lingiari, 200 Aboriginal workers went on strike and walked off the Wave Hill cattle station demanding equal pay and land rights.

Their action still resonates today, and in the early 1990s was celebrated in the song written by Kev Carmody and Paul Kelly entitled 'From Little Things Big Things Grow'.

The struggle of the Gurindji people inspired the Federal Council for the Advancement of Aborigines and Torres Strait Islanders, which had led the 1967 referendum campaign. It adopted a new community-driven agenda based upon land rights and equal wages. At its annual conference in 1968, the organisation presented this new agenda, stressing that the Crown since 1788 had never offered to make treaties and that Aboriginal people had never been given the opportunity to regain lands that were lost. As Joe McGinness, a Kungarakan man and President of the body, told the conference, 'You can't have a people without land'.[4] Non-Indigenous campaigner Jack Horner – a veteran of the referendum campaign – likewise said: 'No issue united the Aboriginal people so much, and so openly, as that of land rights. They could see it as both an economic base for future independence and a glimmer of hope that they might run their communal affairs without political interference'.[5]

These aspirations for economic development and political power were often driven by stories of autonomy and land rights from overseas. When the National Aborigines Day Observance Committee invited Aboriginal leaders from Canada, the United States and New Zealand to Australia in 1968, the visit drew media scrutiny because of the stark contrast between the treaties negotiated in those other nations and the ongoing struggle for land rights at home.

In 1971, Aboriginal demands for land rights took a dramatic turn when the Yolngu people sought an injunction in the Supreme Court of the Northern Territory against mining company Nabalco and the Commonwealth to stop mining at Gove. Later that year, Justice Blackburn rejected their claim to land rights. He found that their customary land laws were not supported by the Australian legal system, leaving the Yolngu 'deeply shocked'.[6] It was little consolation that Justice Blackburn observed that 'the evidence shows a subtle and elaborate system highly adapted to the country ... if ever a system could be called "a government of laws, and not of men", it is that shown in the evidence before me'.[7] As far as the Yolngu were concerned, 'The Australian law has said that the land is not ours. This is not so. It might be right legally but ... morally it's wrong. The law must be changed'.[8]

The Gove decision intensified Aboriginal demands for land rights. In the twilight of a 23-year-long conservative rule, Prime Minister McMahon, in an Australia Day speech in 1972, rejected their claims. Instead, 50-year pastoral leases were offered to those groups who 'could make reasonable economic use of the land'.[9] This rejection of land rights was viewed by many Aboriginal people as a clear message: they were 'effectively aliens in their own land'.[10] The government's answer activated a powerful political reaction from a group of Aboriginal activists, who formed an Aboriginal Tent Embassy opposite what is now Old Parliament House in Canberra. Their protest continues to the present day, and at the time raised public and political consciousness for land rights. It was also aimed at influencing the Labor Opposition led by Gough Whitlam. The message was clear: Aboriginal and Torres Strait Islander peoples were frustrated by the lack of meaningful change in their lives as a result of the 1967 referendum.

The election of the Whitlam government in 1972 ushered in a new era of Indigenous law and policy. The government adopted the principle of self-determination – the right of people to freely determine their political, economic and cultural destiny – as underpinning its policy in Indigenous affairs. In its short time in office, the government established the first Department of Aboriginal Affairs and many other initiatives aimed at improving the plight of Aboriginal and Torres Strait Islander peoples.

Whitlam also ratified the International Convention on the Elimination of All Forms of Racial Discrimination, which the federal Parliament then enacted into Australian law via the *Racial Discrimination Act 1975*. This Act was to become a powerful tool for Aboriginal and other peoples in the fight against racism. Whitlam also used the constitutional authority granted by the Australian people in 1967 to establish Aboriginal legal and medical services.

Whitlam set up a royal commission headed by Justice Woodward in 1973 to examine ways to recognise Aboriginal land rights. In response to its recommendations for broad-ranging recognition of such rights in the Northern Territory, Whitlam handed back the title deeds to Lingiari. While pouring the red Daguragu soil into the hands of Lingiari, Whitlam declared:

> Vincent Lingiari, I solemnly hand to you these deeds as proof in Australian law that these lands belong to the Gurindji people, and I put into your hands part of the earth itself as a sign that this land will be the possession of you and your children forever.[11]

The Bill for land rights in the Northern Territory had been introduced into Parliament, but lapsed following the dismissal of the Whitlam government on 11 November 1975. It was passed as the *Aboriginal Land Rights Act (Northern Territory) Act 1976* after the Fraser government took office.

In 1977, the Fraser government moved to create a new representative body for Aboriginal and Torres Strait Islander peoples called the National Aboriginal Conference (NAC). The NAC, like its predecessor the Federal Council for the Advancement of Aborigines and Torres Strait Islanders, adopted an agenda that reflected the aspirations of the Indigenous community: land rights and a treaty.

Treaty and land rights

A recurring theme of Aboriginal advocacy from the years after British settlement has been a desire for a treaty between the state and Indigenous peoples. In 1835, John Batman had negotiated a treaty with the Aboriginal people of Port Phillip District in Victoria, although the treaty was disregarded by the Victorian government. Historian Henry Reynolds also tells the story of GA Robinson negotiating an 'oral treaty' with Aboriginal people in Tasmania. These aside, no treaties were negotiated between Indigenous peoples and the state at the time of colonisation. By contrast, the British made treaties with Indigenous peoples in other places, such as the Treaty of Waitangi in New Zealand and the many treaties reached in Canada and the United States.

A treaty has been viewed as a way of reaching a broad

settlement between Indigenous and non-Indigenous Australians to facilitate the participation of Aboriginal people in the political system. It could also resolve 'unfinished business' such as land rights. The idea has attracted support not only from Aboriginal people, but also the broader Australian community. Around the time the NAC was established, a coalition of non-Indigenous Australians was formed to support the negotiation of a treaty. The members of the Aboriginal Treaty Committee included prominent Australians such as renowned anthropologist and public servant Nugget Coombs and poet Judith Wright.

In 1979, the NAC led nationwide consultations with Aboriginal and Torres Strait Islander communities on a treaty. Following this, the NAC formally announced its call for a Treaty of Commitment to be negotiated between Aboriginal people and the Commonwealth. This coincided with a decision by Justice Harry Gibbs of the High Court rejecting a claim to Aboriginal sovereignty by Wiradjuri man Paul Coe. Coe had unsuccessfully argued that Captain Cook, Arthur Phillip and British settlement 'wrongfully treated the continent now known as Australia as terra nullius whereas it was occupied by the sovereign Aboriginal nation', and that 'the Aboriginal people ... were entitled not to be dispossessed ... without bilateral treaty, lawful compensation and/or lawful international intervention'.[12]

The Fraser government replied to the NAC's call for a treaty by committing to future discussions. Following feedback from the Minister for Aboriginal Affairs, Fred Chaney, about the potential for the word 'treaty' to alienate ordinary Australians, the NAC resolved to replace the word 'treaty' with Makarrata, a Yolngu word meaning 'things are all right again after a conflict' or 'coming together after a struggle'.[13] The NAC then travelled around Australia to speak with Indigenous peoples about a treaty. Its interim report reflected concerns about sovereignty, the recognition of customary laws and land rights. It also suggested measures to increase Indigenous participation in Australian political life, including the reservation of seats in federal and state parliaments and local government bodies. Other proposals included the repatriation of human remains and the teaching of Aboriginal culture in schools. In early 1981, the Fraser government and the NAC exchanged letters about a Makarrata, in which the former encouraged the NAC to commence negotiations with the states and territories.

One of the final acts of the Fraser government was to constitute a Senate Standing Committee on Legal and Constitutional Affairs to examine the feasibility of securing a compact or Makarrata between the Commonwealth and Aboriginal peoples. Its 1983 report *Two Hundred Years Later ...* recommended that the government consider a treaty in consultation with Aboriginal people. As to the preferred method of implementation, the Committee recommended the insertion into the Constitution of a provision 'which would confer a broad power on the Commonwealth to enter into a compact with representatives of the Aboriginal people'.[14]

The NAC's campaign for a treaty was hampered by many factors, including a lack of funding, tension in the Indigenous community over the logistics of negotiating a treaty, and a dispute with the non-Indigenous Aboriginal Treaty Committee. The final straw came with the election of Prime Minister Bob Hawke in 1983. Treaty advocacy petered out as the NAC was abolished by the incoming government, which instead proposed to realise another aspect of the Aboriginal political agenda, a national Aboriginal land rights framework.

Hawke was elected at a time when Australia was turning its attention to the upcoming bicentenary of British settlement in 1988. In preparation, the government established a commission to undertake a review of the Australian Constitution. The members of the Commission included some of Australia's most distinguished politicians and jurists, such as Sir Maurice Byers, Enid Campbell, Sir Rupert Hamer, Gough Whitlam and Leslie Zines.

The final report of the Constitutional Commission was delivered in 1988 and contained several recommendations relating to Aboriginal and Torres Strait Islander peoples. These included the deletion of section 25 of the Constitution, arguing that it was 'no longer appropriate to include in the Constitution a provision which contemplates the disqualification of members of a race from voting'.[15] In addition, the report raised concerns about the races power as amended in the 1967 referendum. The Commission noted that the wording of the section permits the Parliament to pass both 'special and discriminating laws'. It recommended deleting the power because:

> Australia has joined the many nations which have rejected race as a legitimate criterion on which legislation can be based. The attitudes now officially adopted to discrimination on the basis of race are in striking contrast to those which motivated the Framers of the Constitution. It is appropriate that the change in attitude be reflected.[16]

The Commission recommended that the races power be replaced with a new power authorising the Parliament to make laws with respect to 'Aborigines and Torres Strait Islanders'. It also proposed the insertion of a clause that would prevent this and other powers being used to discriminate against any person on the basis of their race.

A treaty was also on the Commission's agenda. The body looked in particular at the 1983 Senate Committee's idea of a federal power to enter into such agreements. The Commission recommended that such a clause be inserted into the Constitution, but that this not be open to use until a treaty had been negotiated and concluded. While the Commission recommended against a treaty at that time, it commented:

> There is no doubt that the Commonwealth has sufficient constitutional powers to take appropriate action to assist in the promotion of reconciliation with Aboriginal and Torres Strait Island citizens and to recognise their special place in the Commonwealth of Australia. Whether an agreement, or a number of agreements, is an appropriate way of working to that objective has yet to be determined.[17]

As the country celebrated the bicentenary, so too did the Indigenous community commemorate the dispossession of their lands. Aboriginal people declared a 'Year of Mourning' and activists penned the slogan 'White Australia has a Black History'. On 19 January 1988, the *Sydney Morning Herald* observed that 'scarcely a day of the Bicentenary has passed when issues involving Aborigines and their "Year of Mourning" protests have not featured prominently'.[18] On 26 January 1988, when over two million Australians gathered to celebrate the bicentenary, more than 40 000 people, including Aborigines from across the country and non-Indigenous supporters, staged what was the largest march in Sydney since the Vietnam War. Historians Peter Cochrane and David Goodman wrote:

> From the beginning, the Bicentenary has been contested ground … The most profound challenge to the official construction of the event to be celebrated has come from Aboriginal groups. Perhaps not since the mid-nineteenth century has the basic question of [the] right to occupy the continent been posed with such clarity, and received such mainstream attention.[19]

On 12 June that year, a special meeting of Aboriginal people took place in Barunga, Northern Territory. In the years leading up to the bicentenary, the leaders of the major Aboriginal land councils, including Galarrwuy Yunupingu, Wenten Rubuntja and Patrick Dodson and other Aboriginal leaders, had worked on a petition of political claims. The Barunga Statement was inspired by the Yirrkala Bark Petitions sent to the Parliament in 1963 objecting to mining on Yolngu country. The Barunga demands were typed and affixed to a bark painting depicting many of the Northern Territory clans, including Yolngu and the Central Desert. The Statement called for recognition of Aboriginal rights and for the federal Parliament to pass laws providing for:

- A national elected Aboriginal and Islander organisation to oversee Aboriginal and Islander affairs;

- A national system of land rights;
- A police and justice system which recognises our customary laws and frees us from discrimination and any activity which may threaten our identity or security, interfere with our freedom of expression or association, or otherwise prevent our full enjoyment and exercise of universally recognised human rights and fundamental freedoms.[20]

The Statement also called upon the Commonwealth to 'negotiate with us a Treaty recognising our prior ownership, continued occupation and sovereignty and affirming our human rights and freedom.'[21]

The Statement was presented personally to the Prime Minister in 1988. In reply, Hawke declared that there would be a treaty within the life of the current Parliament, saying:

> There shall be a treaty negotiated between the Aboriginal people and the Government on behalf of all the people of Australia ... these processes should start before the end of this year and ... we would expect and hope and work for the conclusion of such a treaty before the end of the life of this Parliament.[22]

Hawke delivered on only one of the demands presented to him by the Barunga Statement: a new elected representative body. Following an extensive consultation period that included 500 meetings with 14500 people (including 6000 personal discussions between Minister Gerry Hand and Aboriginal and Torres Strait Islander people), the federal Parliament created an independent statutory body called the Aboriginal and Torres Strait Islander Commission (ATSIC) in 1989.

By the time he was deposed as Prime Minister by Paul Keating, Hawke had neither negotiated a treaty nor had Parliament legislated for national land rights. Days after abandoning a uniform national land rights package, the Prime Minister told the National Press Club that 'Australians as a whole weren't as compassionate as they were in 1967, when the Federal Government was given power over Aboriginal affairs'.[23] In an interview on ABC Television's *Four Corners,* Patrick Dodson said that 'Aboriginal people view the spirit of the '67 Referendum going down the drain'.[24]

Reflecting the frustrations of the time, the song 'Treaty' was written by Yothu Yindi in collaboration with Paul Kelly and Midnight Oil, capturing the sense of anticipation at the commitment that there would be a treaty and disappointment at the failure to honour it.[25]

Hawke's failure to deliver on the issues most important to Aboriginal and Torres Strait Islander peoples signalled the next phase on the journey to constitutional reform: reconciliation. Reconciliation was conceived by Hawke as a political solution to broken promises and the perennial demands for land rights and a treaty.

Reconciliation

Australia's decade of 'reconciliation' commenced in 1991, when the federal Parliament enacted a law establishing the Council for Aboriginal Reconciliation. The *Council for Aboriginal*

Reconciliation Act 1991 acknowledged that there had been 'no formal process of reconciliation between Aborigines and Torres Strait Islanders and other Australians'.[26] The reaction was mixed. Many Indigenous people were dismayed at the slide from a treaty to what they saw as 'a somewhat desultory reconciliation process'.[27] This included Aboriginal poet Kevin Gilbert, who felt that 'the reconciliation process can achieve nothing because it does not at the end of the day promise justice'.[28]

Even so, the preamble to the Act contained some weighty notions, including that 'Australia was occupied by Aborigines and Torres Strait Islanders who had settled for thousands of years, before British settlement at Sydney Cove on 26 January 1788', and that 'many Aborigines and Torres Strait Islanders suffered dispossession and dispersal from their traditional lands by the British Crown'.[29] In addition, the Council included a broad membership from across the community. Its co-chairs were Evelyn Scott, a Torres Strait Islander, and scientist Sir Gustav Nossal.

The purpose of the Council was to lead a national process of reconciliation leading up to the Centenary of Federation in 2001. The three goals of Council were to create formal documents of reconciliation, develop partnerships based upon reconciliation and build a people's movement for reconciliation. Each required the Council to lead a nationwide consultative process to seek the views of all Australians and raise public awareness of reconciliation. The reconciliation movement, led by the Council, grew during the 1990s and was boosted by gestures such as the 1992 Redfern speech delivered by Prime Minister Paul Keating. He acknowledged the history of

Australia and the wrongs committed against Aboriginal people by the colonisers:

> It was we who did the dispossessing.
>
> We took the traditional lands and smashed the traditional way of life.
>
> We brought the diseases and the alcohol. We committed the murders.
>
> We took the children from their mothers ...
>
> We failed to ask – how would I feel if this were done to me?[30]

That same year, the High Court of Australia handed down its decision in *Mabo*.[31] It was the culmination of a ten-year legal struggle by the Meriam people seeking rights to the use and enjoyment of their traditional lands in the Torres Strait. The action had been commenced by five Murray Islanders, including Eddie Mabo. The question asked by the Murray Islanders was whether, on acquiring sovereignty, the Crown had gained complete ownership of the land, or whether it was burdened by any prior Aboriginal title. The Court rejected the idea that Australia was terra nullius, or no man's land, at the time of British settlement. It held as a result that the pre-existing native title rights of Indigenous peoples continued to exist.

Following the *Mabo* decision, Keating negotiated a three-part response to address the dispossession of Aboriginal and

Torres Strait Islander peoples. These were the *Native Title Act 1993*, the Indigenous Land Corporation, and a Social Justice Package to compensate Indigenous peoples who had been dispossessed and unable to claim native title.

An ATSIC committee led by Charles Perkins and the Australian Human Rights Commission's Aboriginal and Torres Strait Islander Social Justice Commissioner Mick Dodson led consultations with the Aboriginal and Torres Strait Islander community on an appropriate social justice response to the High Court's landmark decision in *Mabo*. In *Mabo*, native title was found to have survived the assertion of Crown law by the Commonwealth. The ATSIC committee published and submitted to the Prime Minister a report entitled 'Recognition, Rights and Reform', which reaffirmed community aspirations to constitutional recognition in light of *Mabo*: 'the Commonwealth Government should note that the national consultation process in relation to the Social Justice Package showed overwhelming support for the reform of the Constitution especially in relation to recognition of Indigenous peoples'.

The Social Justice Package reforms included suggestions that the federal Parliament use the power it gained in the 1967 referendum to initiate major institutional and structural changes, such as regional self-government and regional agreements, and the negotiation of a treaty or comparable document addressing the issue of compensation.

At this point, the process floundered. Keating lost the 1996 election to the Liberal–National Coalition led by John Howard. The new government abandoned the Social Justice Package, meaning that this third pillar of the *Mabo* response was never delivered.

The Howard era

There were more setbacks to come during the 1990s. In particular, two High Court decisions led to a deep divide between Aboriginal people and the government, and an often bitter political debate. The first decision in *Wik* related to native title, the second in the *Hindmarsh Island Bridge Case* to the unintended consequences of the 1967 referendum.

On 23 December 1996, the High Court handed down the *Wik* decision, which held that pastoral leases do not necessarily extinguish native title. The Howard government responded with the *Native Title Amendment Act 1998*. It implemented a 'ten point plan' that, in the words of Deputy Prime Minister Tim Fischer, sought to pour 'bucket-loads of extinguishment'[32] on the native title rights of Indigenous Australians. To wind back these native title rights, the *Native Title Amendment Act 1998* suspended the operation of the *Racial Discrimination Act*. This cleared the way for the law to adversely discriminate against Aboriginal native title claimants by reducing their rights in favour of the rights of others.

During the negotiations for the *Wik* amendments, another challenge to reconciliation emerged. On 26 May 1997, the Human Rights and Equal Opportunity Commission tabled the *Bringing Them Home* report. Initiated during the Keating government, the Inquiry examined the former practice of separating Aboriginal and Torres Strait Islander children from their families. One of the chief recommendations was an apology to those Stolen Generations. However, Prime Minister Howard opposed an apology because he believed that Australians 'should not be required to accept guilt and blame for past actions and policies over which they had no control'.[33] He said that, 'if I have not been part of any wrongdoing and if I'm not part of a generation that's been part of that wrongdoing, I've always had a difficulty in assuming responsibility for the claimed wrongdoings of earlier generations, particularly when those acts were sanctioned by the law of the country'.[34]

The Prime Minister's position was a source of tension between him and Indigenous peoples throughout his time in government. During Howard's speech to the Australian Reconciliation Convention in 1997, many attendees stood up and turned their backs in protest that he refused to say sorry to the Stolen Generations. It was not until his second term of office that on 26 August 1999 he introduced a Motion of Reconciliation into Parliament, which had been developed in consultation with Aboriginal Senator Aden Ridgeway, a member of the Democrats. The Motion expressed its 'deep and sincere regret that Indigenous Australians suffered injustices under the practices of past generations, and for the hurt and trauma that many Indigenous people continue to feel as a consequence of those practices'.[35] The Motion was criticised by Aboriginal and Torres Strait Islander people because of the Prime Minister's insistence on using the word 'regret' instead of 'sorry'. The use of the former word was regarded as being insincere.

The second High Court decision came in 1998. One of the Howard government's first acts when it came to power in 1996 had been to shepherd legislation through Parliament, relying on the races power, to prevent the Ngarrindjeri Aboriginal women in South Australia from invoking the *Aboriginal and Torres Strait Islander Heritage Protection Act 1984* to stop the construction of a bridge over an area where they engaged in secret women's business. The *Hindmarsh Island Bridge Act 1997* restricted the operation of the *Heritage Protection Act* so that it applied everywhere in Australia except for the Hindmarsh Island bridge area.

This legislation was challenged by the Ngarrindjeri women in the High Court on the basis that the races power – as amended in 1967 – cannot be used in an adverse or detrimental manner by the Commonwealth. The Commonwealth responded by arguing that there are no limits on the power so long as the law imposed a consequence based on race.

Effectively, the Commonwealth was arguing that it could use the races power to pass discriminatory laws. Lest there was any doubt about this, the Commonwealth's lawyer, Gavan Griffith, said to the High Court that the races power 'is infected, the power is infused with a power of adverse operation'. He also acknowledged its 'direct racist content', in the sense of 'a capacity for adverse operation'. This prompted the following exchange between Justice Michael Kirby of the High Court and Griffith:

> JUSTICE KIRBY: Can I just get clear in my mind, is the Commonwealth's submission that it is entirely and exclusively for the Parliament to determine the matter upon which special laws are deemed necessary or whatever the words say or is there a point at which there is a justiciable question for the Court? I mean, it seems unthinkable that a law such as the Nazi race laws could be enacted under the race power and that this Court could do nothing about it.

> MR GRIFFITH: Your Honour, if there was a reason why the Court could do something about it, a Nazi law, it would, in our submission, be for a reason external to the races power. It would be for some wider overarching reason.[36]

On 1 April 1998, the High Court handed down its decision upholding the *Hindmarsh Island Bridge Act*, thereby rejecting the claims of the Ngarrindjeri women. The judgments left open the possibility that the Commonwealth can use the races power to impose racially discriminatory laws upon Aboriginal people.

This decision was a turning point in post-1967 Aboriginal advocacy. The prospect that the federal Parliament had gained a power to discriminate against Aboriginal people was alarming. This caught the attention of the United Nations committee tasked to monitor domestic implementation of the treaty upon which the *Racial Discrimination Act* was based. The Committee on the Elimination of All Forms of Racial Discrimination was so disturbed by these developments that it placed Australia on its early warning urgent action list, the first Western country to be so named.

By 1998, although Aboriginal people continued to call for the negotiation of a treaty, the debate had shifted considerably. The emergence of a national conversation about Australia becoming a republic led to prominence being given to the question of how to acknowledge Indigenous peoples if Australia was to make that shift. During his first term, Howard convened a ten-day Constitutional Convention at Old Parliament House in Canberra in February 1998 to consider whether Australia should become a republic, and to debate the model.

The Convention comprised 152 delegates, half of whom

were elected and half who were parliamentary representatives and government appointees. One issue at the Convention was whether the move to a republic should also bring with it a new preamble, or opening words, to the Constitution. Chairman of the Australian Republican Movement, Malcolm Turnbull, argued that if a preamble 'is to remain a statement of history, then it should pay appropriate regard and respect to Aboriginal history'.[37] The Convention recommended that a new preamble to the Constitution provide explicit 'acknowledgement of the original occupancy and custodianship of Australia by Aboriginal peoples and Torres Strait Islanders', and 'recognition that Aboriginal people and Torres Strait Islanders have continuing rights by virtue of their status as Australia's indigenous peoples'.[38]

The focus on a preamble reflected a significant shift in thinking. It involved a move away from considering more substantial forms of recognition, such as giving legal force to rights to land, to symbolic recognition in the Constitution. At the time, Indigenous peoples were reassured by the fact that the Council for Aboriginal Reconciliation was continuing its work towards developing a roadmap for reconciliation that could include such substantive measures. Nevertheless, the Council cautioned that a new preamble carried dangers because it might 'be seen as an easy symbolic step which would be all that was needed to address constitutional issues for Indigenous peoples'.[39]

Prime Minister Howard took the lead in drafting the new preamble. In March 1999, he engaged poet Les Murray to co-write the text. The Howard–Murray preamble read:

With hope in God, the Commonwealth of Australia is constituted by the equal sovereignty of all its citizens.

The Australian nation is woven together of people from many ancestries and arrivals.

Our vast island continent has helped to shape the destiny of our Commonwealth and the spirit of its people.

Since time immemorial our land has been inhabited by Aborigines and Torres Strait Islanders, who are honoured for their ancient and continuing cultures.

In every generation immigrants have brought great enrichment to our nation's life.

Australians are free to be proud of their country and heritage, free to realise themselves as individuals, and free to pursue their hopes and ideals.

We value excellence as well as fairness, independence as dearly as mateship.

Australia's democratic and federal system of government exists under law to preserve and protect all Australians in an equal dignity which may never be infringed by prejudice or fashion or ideology nor invoked against achievement.

In this spirit we, the Australian people, commit ourselves to this Constitution.[40]

This version was widely ridiculed, in part because of its reference to 'mateship'. The reference to Aboriginal and Torres Strait Islander peoples was also panned by Indigenous leaders, including Michael Mansell, Peter Yu, Lowitja O'Donoghue and Gatjil Djerrkura. They regarded it as failing to go beyond recognition of prior occupation and criticised its failure to use the word 'custodianship' suggested by the Constitutional Convention.

Murray resigned from the process because he felt that his language was being interfered with, stating that, '[t]he preamble has now been compromised away to mush, compromised so much it doesn't matter anymore. I'm not saying that out of peevishness. It went into the political compromise machine and came out mush'.[41] At this point, the Australian Labor Party and the Australian Republic Movement argued for the preamble proposal to be abandoned entirely because they thought it risked diverting attention away from the move to a republic.

The Prime Minister then engaged Democrats Senator Aden Ridgeway to assist him to revise the wording. According to Howard, 'the fact that the two of us have come together … symbolises the value of the preamble as a uniting element in constitutional debate in Australia'.[42] The collaboration led to a new draft that was passed by Parliament and then, along with the proposal for a republic, put to the Australian people at a referendum in 1999. This final version read:

> With hope in God, the Commonwealth of Australia
> is constituted as a democracy with a federal system of
> government to serve the common good.

We the Australian people commit ourselves to this Constitution:

proud that our national unity has been forged by Australians from many ancestries;

never forgetting the sacrifices of all who defended our country and our liberty in time of war;

upholding freedom, tolerance, individual dignity and the rule of law;

honouring Aborigines and Torres Strait Islanders, the nation's first people, for their deep kinship with their lands and for their ancient and continuing cultures which enrich the life of our country;

recognising the nation building contribution of generations of immigrants;

mindful of our responsibility to protect our unique natural environment;

supportive of achievement as well as equality of opportunity for all;

and valuing independence as dearly as the national spirit which binds us together in both adversity and success.[43]

The line acknowledging Aboriginal and Torres Strait Islander peoples was again criticised by Indigenous leaders. It did not adopt the word 'custodianship', which had been put forward by the Constitutional Convention as best describing the Aboriginal connection to land. Rather, the word 'kinship' was used to describe this relationship. For many leaders, 'kinship' did not easily apply to the connection between a person and a place or thing. ATSIC Chairman Gatjil Djerrkura said 'the term "kinship" in my view, is a word that describes personal relationship, people's relationship. It doesn't reflect a relationship to the land. Custodianship, yes'.[44]

Senator Ridgeway replied to critics by saying that their objections were 'too legal or too anthropological'. He said he had grappled with how to capture traditional ownership, stewardship and custodianship in a single word and 'I think that kinship achieves that'.[45] Peter Yu, head of the Kimberley Land Council, disagreed, arguing: '[The preamble] doesn't reflect the fundamental truth ... that we are the original occupiers and owners of this country ... and continue to have existing rights'.[46] More generally, such concerns reflected a lack of consultation with Aboriginal and Torres Strait Islander leaders. When the Prime Minister was asked if he had consulted other Indigenous leaders, he replied that he had not.

Together, Howard and Ridgeway insisted that their preamble would advance the cause of reconciliation because the text of the Constitution otherwise contained no reference to Aboriginal and Torres Strait Islander peoples. Nonetheless, the preamble was soundly rejected by Australian voters. The referendum held on 6 November 1999 saw the preamble rejected by every state and territory, and nationally it attracted a No vote of 60.7 per cent (a significantly worse result than that for the republic, which was also defeated). The rejection was pronounced in electorates with Aboriginal and Torres Strait Islander populations.

On celebrating the preamble's failure, poet Murray joked that 'the Australian people had mercifully taken it out the back and shot it'.[47] For Djerrkura, the preamble 'did not promote reconciliation or advance our aspirations. I welcome its resounding defeat'. In addition he said the process of drafting the preamble lacked 'proper consultation' with Indigenous people.[48]

A feature of the failed preamble was the inclusion of a clause recommended by the Constitutional Convention that provided that the preamble could have no legal effect. This was expressed in proposed clause 125A, which provided that 'the preamble to this Constitution has no legal force and shall not be considered in interpreting this Constitution or the law in force in the Commonwealth or any part of the Commonwealth'.[49] This clause was designed to placate those who feared that the High Court might use a new preamble to infer new rights from the Constitution, such as in regard to the interests of Aboriginal people. Others saw the clause as suggesting insincerity, or as being excessive and alarmist, not least because the High Court has historically treated the existing preamble in the Constitution 'with a mix of indifference and reticence'.[50]

The results of reconciliation

Following the failed referendum, the nation moved towards the final chapter of the reconciliation era. A decade after its creation, the Council for Aboriginal Reconciliation finally delivered its *Roadmap for Reconciliation*. This contained the National Strategy for Recognising Aboriginal and Torres Strait Islander Peoples' Rights, which recommended that a referendum be held to change the Constitution to:

- recognise Aboriginal and Torres Strait Islander peoples as the first peoples of Australia in a new preamble to the Constitution; and
- remove section 25 of the Constitution and introduce a new section making it unlawful to adversely discriminate against any people on the grounds of race.[51]

The Council's recommendations, addressed to Prime Minister Howard, also included that 'the Commonwealth Parliament enact legislation ... to put in place a process which will unite all Australians by way of an agreement, or treaty, through which unresolved issues of reconciliation can be resolved'.[52] By these recommendations, the Council reinforced Aboriginal and Torres Strait Islander aspirations for a treaty and echoed the Constitutional Commission's call for a racial non-discrimination clause.

On 27 May 2000, at an event called Corroboree 2000, the Council presented the *Australian Declaration towards Reconciliation* and the *Roadmap for Reconciliation* to the Australian people and the Prime Minister. The reconciliation documents arrived at the Man O' War steps outside the Sydney Opera House aboard the vessel *Tribal Warrior*. The documents were met with a smoking ceremony before being carried in a procession into the Opera House. Governor-General Sir William Deane told the audience:

> It's wrong to see those past injustices as belonging, as it were, to another country … they have been absorbed into the present and the future of contemporary Indigenous Australians and of the nation of which they form such an important part. They – and the land that was taken – are our country.[53]

The next day, the Council delivered spectacularly on its other goal to 'build a people's movement toward reconciliation',[54] when one million people walked in capital cities and towns in support of reconciliation. This gesture, known as the Bridge Walks, reflected the years that the Council had spent raising awareness of the importance of reconciliation to the future of the nation. The Sydney leg of the Bridge Walk saw 300 000 people walk across the Sydney Harbour Bridge. It was reported that the Sydney march started just after 8 am, 'behind the golf buggies carrying Indigenous elders from across Australia'. According to one newspaper report, some 25 000 Sydneysiders walked in the first timeslot, and 'many of them walked in silence. Some cried … It was an extraordinary display of harmony and togetherness'.[55]

While the Council's efforts were a political response to Hawke's broken promises, the Bridge Walks demonstrated what could be achieved in raising community consciousness through leadership and an orchestrated campaign. The success of the Bridge Walks also suggested that political sentiment was out of touch with the public's desire to reconcile with Australia's first peoples. The day after the Bridge Walks, the Prime Minister, who had refused to participate in the walks, dismissed the Council's recommendation for a treaty. He said that, 'a nation ... does not make a treaty with itself'.[56]

Despite Howard's opposition to a treaty, on 8 November 2000, the *Sydney Morning Herald* reported an increase in the number of Australians who supported this outcome. The Herald–ACNielsen poll found 53 per cent of Australians were in favour of a treaty, 'with those opposed dropping 6 per cent to 34 per cent over the previous poll in June'.[57] The poll also found that support for reconciliation had risen from 74 per cent to 78 per cent.

The work towards a treaty passed over to the leadership of ATSIC, which picked up where the Council and NAC had left off. ATSIC hoped to build upon the final report of the Council for Aboriginal Reconciliation, which had called on governments to:

> recognise that this land and its waters were settled as colonies without treaty or consent, and that to advance reconciliation it would be most desirable if there were agreements or treaties, and to negotiate a process through which this might be achieved that protects the political, legal, cultural and economic position of Aboriginal and Torres Strait Islander peoples.[58]

ATSIC's intent was not to negotiate a treaty, but to provide information and to facilitate a process that would allow the Indigenous community to negotiate a treaty with the state. However, this collided with the Prime Minister's agenda of 'practical reconciliation'.

Howard created an artificial dichotomy between practical and symbolic reconciliation. He characterised the issues to be focused on as socio-economic disadvantage such as housing, education, employment and health, as opposed to symbolism, which he equated with substantive rights. He reinforced his long-held rejection of symbolic reconciliation when, in the wake of the failed 1999 referendum, he said that reconciliation in the form of Indigenous rights, a treaty, Stolen Generations and deaths in custody had failed.

One consequence of this was the demise of ATSIC itself. With the support of the Australian Labor Party, Parliament passed a law in 2004 that abolished the body. ATSIC Commissioner Steve Gordon suggested that this was designed to stop the treaty process. It has since been argued that the abolition of ATSIC was also to prevent regional autonomy plans devised by ATSIC to enhance the economic development of Indigenous communities.

4

THE JOURNEY TO RECOGNITION

The failure of the 1999 referendum did not end attempts to achieve constitutional recognition of Aboriginal and Torres Strait Islander peoples by way of a preamble or other words. The push for this continued, although initially only in the states. Change is easier to achieve at this level as the states can usually amend their constitutions by way of an ordinary Act of Parliament, thereby avoiding the need for a referendum.

Victoria was the first to amend its Constitution to bring this about. It did so in 2004 by inserting the following as a new section 1A:

> **Recognition of Aboriginal people**
> (1) The Parliament acknowledges that the events described in the Preamble to this Act occurred without proper consultation, recognition or involvement of the Aboriginal people of Victoria.
> (2) The Parliament recognises that Victoria's Aboriginal people, as the original custodians of the land on which the Colony of Victoria was established –
>> (a) have a unique status as the descendants of Australia's first people; and
>> (b) have a spiritual, social, cultural and economic relationship with their traditional lands and waters within Victoria; and

> (c) have made a unique and irreplaceable contribution to the identity and well-being of Victoria.[1]

This section comes after the existing preamble to that Constitution, which recites things such as the creation of the self-governing colony of Victoria in 1854.

Queensland, New South Wales and South Australia followed suit. However, Indigenous people expressed strong concern about the recognition provided, as the added words are in each case accompanied by what is known as a non-justiciability clause. For example, the words recognising Aboriginal people in the South Australian Constitution are accompanied by a clause stating that 'the Parliament does not intend this section to have any legal force or effect'.[2]

As with the attempt in 1999 to insert a similar clause into the Australian Constitution, the effect was to undermine Indigenous support because of a perception that this limited recognition is insincere. When the final states of Western Australia and Tasmania changed their constitutions to recognise their Indigenous populations, they did not see such a clause as being necessary. They chose instead to include unfettered words of acknowledgment.

Facing defeat at the 2007 general election, Prime Minister Howard once again expressed his support for recognising Indigenous Australians in the Constitution by way of symbolic change. He announced three days prior to the vote:

> I announce that, if re-elected, I will put to the Australian people within eighteen months a referendum to formally recognise Indigenous Australians in our Constitution –

> their history as the first inhabitants of our country, their unique heritage of culture and languages, and their special (though not separate) place within a reconciled, indivisible nation.
>
> My goal is to see a new Statement of Reconciliation incorporated into the Preamble of the Australian Constitution. If elected, I would commit immediately to working in consultation with Indigenous leaders and others on this task …
>
> I would aim to introduce a [B]ill that would include the Preamble Statement into Parliament within the first 100 days of a new government.
>
> A future referendum question would stand alone. It would not be blurred or cluttered by other constitutional considerations. I would seek to enlist wide community support for a 'Yes' vote. I would hope and aim to secure the sort of overwhelming vote achieved 40 years ago at the 1967 referendum. If approached in the right spirit, I believe this is both realistic and achievable.[3]

Given the timing, the proposal was met with scepticism, not least because Howard confirmed that, once again, he had consulted only one Aboriginal leader. Nevertheless, his speech was an olive branch of sorts given the difficult relationship he had had with Indigenous peoples during his term of office.

An Apology and the Expert Panel

One of the first acts of newly elected Prime Minister Kevin Rudd was to issue an Apology to Australia's Stolen Generations. Rudd's speech on 13 February 2008 distinguished itself from Howard's Motion of Reconciliation by using the word 'sorry':

> For the pain, suffering and hurt of these Stolen Generations, their descendants and for their families left behind, we say sorry.
>
> To the mothers and the fathers, the brothers and the sisters, for the breaking up of families and communities, we say sorry.
>
> And for the indignity and degradation thus inflicted on a proud people and a proud culture, we say sorry.[4]

This was a powerful statement by the Prime Minister on behalf of the Parliament of Australia. It was received with great emotion and joy by Aboriginal and Torres Strait Islander peoples, many of whom declared that for the first time in their lives they felt Australian. In making the apology, Rudd also touched upon the 'constitutional recognition of the first Australians',[5] saying that he wanted to maintain bipartisan support for the idea.

Constitutional recognition was back on the agenda again in April 2008 when the Prime Minister hosted the Australia 2020 Summit to generate ideas for building a modern Australia. One of the streams was 'Options for the Future of Indigenous Australia'. A key outcome of this stream was support for a new national dialogue on reconciliation and the formal legal recognition of Indigenous peoples. In particular, the final report noted the 'strong view that recognition of Aboriginal and Torres Strait Islander peoples' rights needs to be included in the body of the Constitution, not just in the Preamble'.[6]

In the 'Governance' stream of the Summit, Indigenous issues were also raised in relation to the theme of constitution, rights and responsibilities. This stream recommended as its top priority that the Constitution be amended to include a preamble that formally recognises the traditional custodians of Australian land and waters, that the Constitution be amended to remove any language that is racially discriminatory, and that a national process be conducted to consider a compact of reconciliation between Indigenous and non-Indigenous Australians.

Following the 2020 Summit, a community cabinet was held in eastern Arnhem Land on 23 July. Prime Minister Rudd was presented with a Statement of Intent from Yolngu and Bininj Leaders, a document in which members of those communities expressed their desire for constitutional protection for traditional land and cultural rights. The communiqué was written on behalf of Yolngu and Bininj clans living in the Yirrkala, Gunyangara, Gapuwiyak, Maningrida, Galiwin'ku, Milingimbi, Ramingining and Laynhapuy homelands, constituting approximately 8000 Indigenous people in Arnhem Land. It had been developed over 18 months in meetings at Maningrida in western Arnhem Land.

The communiqué was handed to the Prime Minister by Yolngu and Bininj people, who stated they had been 'marginalised and demeaned over the past decade and [had] been denied real opportunity to have a say about [their] aspirations and futures'.[7] They argued for the preconditions for economic and community development in remote communities, including the right to be recognised as maintaining their culture and identity, and protection of their land and sea estates. They also argued for the importance of recognising their right to live on their land and practise their culture, and requested that the Australian government 'work towards constitutional recognition of our prior ownership and rights'.[8]

In accepting this communiqué, Rudd pledged his support for recognition of Indigenous peoples in the Constitution. He said that there was

> nothing new about the fact that the national platform of the Australian Labor Party has said for some time that we've committed to the constitutional recognition of the first Australians. That is not new; it's been around for a long time. That remains our commitment.[9]

In response, opposition leader Dr Brendan Nelson offered bipartisan support for an amended preamble to recognise 'the place of Indigenous people in Australian life'.[10] His comments were consistent with the Liberal Party's 2007 election platform and former Prime Minister Howard's pledge just before the federal election of that year.

At the time, it was widely reported and assumed by the media and political leaders that any constitutional recognition of Indigenous Australians would come in the form of a new preamble. However, the idea that recognition required no more than this neglected the broader aspirations of Aboriginal people, and was based on a misreading of the Yolngu/Bininj

Statement of Intent. That document had, for example, also argued for recognition of land rights.

It sought substantive constitutional rights, not symbolism. After 50 years of advocacy, the goals and aspirations of Aboriginal and Torres Strait Islander peoples continued to be cherry-picked by political parties and the media. Even when Indigenous peoples have called for substantive constitutional recognition, politicians often heard 'symbolic' recognition. This has meant, too often, that constitutional reform has been understood as being synonymous with minimal change such as new opening words to the Constitution.

Due to a leadership spill in the Labor Party, Julia Gillard, rather than Rudd, led the government to the 2010 federal election. That vote resulted in a hung Parliament. Gillard was able to retain her position as Prime Minister by securing the support of Greens and Independent members. In return, she made a number of policy commitments, including holding a referendum during the life of the Parliament or at the next election on Indigenous constitutional recognition.

At the end of 2010, Prime Minister Gillard established an Expert Panel to report on possible options to give effect to Indigenous constitutional recognition and to advise on the level of support from Indigenous people and the broader community for each option. The Panel was led by Professor Patrick Dodson, former Chairman of the Council for Aboriginal Reconciliation, and Mark Leibler, former Reconciliation Australia co-chair. The panel's membership was half Indigenous and half non-Indigenous, selected after a public nomination process. Members included representatives of each of Australia's major parties, as well as people such as Noel Pearson, Marcia Langton,

Expert Panel's recommendations for changes to the Constitution[12]

The Panel recommends:

1. That section 25 be repealed.
2. That section 51(xxvi) be repealed.
3. That a new 'section 51A' be inserted, along the following lines:

Section 51A Recognition of Aboriginal and Torres Strait Islander peoples

Recognising that the continent and its islands now known as Australia were first occupied by Aboriginal and Torres Strait Islander peoples;

Acknowledging the continuing relationship of Aboriginal and Torres Strait Islander peoples with their traditional lands and waters;

Respecting the continuing cultures, languages and heritage of Aboriginal and Torres Strait Islander peoples;

Acknowledging the need to secure the advancement of Aboriginal and Torres Strait Islander peoples;

the Parliament shall, subject to this Constitution, have power to make laws for the peace, order and good government of the Commonwealth with respect to Aboriginal and Torres Strait Islander peoples.

The Panel further recommends that the repeal of section 51(xxvi) and the insertion of the new 'section 51A' be proposed together.

4. That a new 'section 116A' be inserted, along the following lines:

Section 116A Prohibition of racial discrimination

(1) The Commonwealth, a State or a Territory shall not discriminate on the grounds of race, colour or ethnic or national origin.

(2) Subsection (1) does not preclude the making of laws or measures for the purpose of overcoming disadvantage, ameliorating the effects of past discrimination, or protecting the cultures, languages or heritage of any group.

5. That a new 'section 127A' be inserted, along the following lines:

Section 127A Recognition of languages

(1) The national language of the Commonwealth of Australia is English.

(3) The Aboriginal and Torres Strait Islander languages are the original Australian languages, a part of our national heritage.

Fred Chaney, and the co-chairs of the National Congress of Australia's First Peoples.

The Expert Panel was charged with leading a national consultation and engagement program to seek the views of a wide spectrum of the community, based on a discussion paper that set out ideas for reform. It travelled the length and breadth of Australia between May and October 2011, holding more than 250 meetings in 84 remote, regional and metropolitan areas. People at these meetings were asked whether the Constitution should be changed and, if so, how. The Panel also published a discussion paper, held a formal public submission process, and produced a website – all of which were aimed at capturing the views of as many people as possible.

The Panel received over 3500 submissions from members of the public, members of Parliament, Aboriginal and Torres Strait

Islander leaders, organisations and individuals, community groups, legal professionals and academics. In developing its proposals for reform, it met with Indigenous leaders across Australia and constitutional law experts. The Panel adopted four principles to guide its assessment of proposals, namely that a proposal must:

1. contribute to a more unified and reconciled nation;
2. be of benefit to and accord with the wishes of Aboriginal and Torres Strait Islander peoples;
3. be capable of being supported by an overwhelming majority of Australians from across the political and social spectrums; and
4. be technically and legally sound.[11]

The Panel's report, released in early 2012, identified strong community support for changing the Constitution to acknowledge Aboriginal and Torres Strait Islander peoples. As set out on the previous page, it recommended specific options for reform, including inserting words of recognition, removing the remaining clauses that enable discrimination on the basis of race and inserting a new clause to protect all people from racial discrimination. These recommendations are discussed in chapter 5.

Acts of recognition

The Gillard government did not respond to the Panel's report, nor did it seek to put any referendum, saying that the political environment was not consistent with maintaining bipartisan support and a referendum might fail due to low levels of community awareness.

Instead, it funded Reconciliation Australia to raise community awareness of the issue. That led to the creation of Recognise, a body funded and supervised by Reconciliation Australia that was actively involved in explaining to Australians what this issue is about, and why they should support reform. Among other things, Recognise initiated a Journey to Recognition relay around the country that by late 2014 had travelled 28 000 kilometres, passing through 188 communities and holding 238 events engaging with over 17 500 people. Recognise was active until 2017, when it was wound down.

In the absence of a referendum, the Gillard government introduced a measure into Parliament to provide an interim form of recognition of Aboriginal people. This law, the *Aboriginal and Torres Strait Islander Peoples Recognition Act 2013*, was passed with the benefit of cross-party support. It incorporates recognition by stating that 'the Parliament, on behalf of the people of Australia, acknowledges the continuing relationship of Aboriginal and Torres Strait Islander peoples with their traditional lands and waters'.[13]

The Act stipulated that the Minister should conduct a review within 12 months to consider the readiness of the Australian public to support a referendum; consider proposals for constitutional change to recognise Aboriginal and Torres Strait Islander peoples, taking into account the work of the Expert Panel and Reconciliation Australia; and identify which of those proposals would be most likely to obtain the support of the Australian people.

This review was also asked to determine the level of support for amending the Constitution to recognise Aboriginal and Torres Strait Islander peoples among Indigenous peoples, the wider Australian public and the governments of the states and territories. The ALP regarded the review as preventing any future Abbott government from letting the issue subside.

The Act was set to lapse in two years (in 2015), on the basis that it was only intended as a stopgap measure until the Constitution was changed. However, in 2015, the Constitution had still not been changed. Parliament therefore passed the *Aboriginal and Torres Strait Islander Peoples Recognition (Sunset Extension) Act 2015*, which replaced the initial two-year lapse period with a five-year period. The Act was finally repealed in 2018.

In a rare example of bipartisanship for the time, opposition leader Tony Abbott spoke strongly in favour of the Act and the idea of constitutional recognition in general. He said:

> Australia is a blessed country. Our climate, our land, our people, our institutions rightly make us the envy of the earth, except for one thing – we have never fully made peace with the First Australians. This is the stain on our soul that Prime Minister Keating so movingly evoked at Redfern 21 years ago. We have to acknowledge that pre-1788 this land was as Aboriginal then as it is Australian now. Until we have acknowledged that, we will be an incomplete nation and a torn people.[14]

He argued that a referendum should be held after the 2013 election, saying:

> I believe that we are equal to this task of completing our Constitution rather than changing it. The next parliament will, I trust, finish the work that this one has begun.[15]

Each of Australia's major parties at the 2013 federal election expressed strong support for recognising Aboriginal peoples in the Constitution. These commitments were, however, light on detail. No party provided a considered response to the options recommended by the Expert Panel. Abbott did, however, express scepticism about the insertion of any clause into the Constitution that might protect people from racial discrimination. He described the Panel's recommendation to this effect as being a 'one-clause Bill of Rights'.[16]

As the victor of the 2013 election, Abbott said that he wanted to be Australia's first 'Prime Minister for Aboriginal Affairs'. Consistent with this, he repeated on several occasions his support for recognising Aboriginal peoples in the Constitution. For example, he said in his 2014 Australia Day address:

> We will also begin a national conversation about amending our Constitution to recognise Aboriginal peoples as the first Australians. This should be another unifying moment in the history of our country.[17]

He also said that his government would release a timetable and concrete proposal for achieving constitutional recognition. The Prime Minister's move was backed by opposition leader Bill Shorten, who said in August 2014 at the Garma Festival in the Northern Territory: 'the sooner our Constitution honours the people who have shared an unbroken connection with this ancient continent – the better'. Shorten also said that constitutional recognition has to involve more than a token gesture: 'We need substantive and substantial change. Symbolic change is not good enough … Many Indigenous people have made it clear to me that they believe banning racism in our Constitution is vital'.[18]

In March 2014, the Coalition government engaged former Deputy Prime Minister and National Party leader John Anderson to conduct the review into public support for constitutional recognition mandated by the Recognition Act. The government said it wanted to 'work towards a parliamentary and community consensus on referendum proposals and report on steps that can be taken to progress towards a successful referendum'. Parliament also formed a joint select parliamentary committee chaired by Indigenous members of Parliament, Liberal Ken Wyatt from Western Australia and Northern Territory Labor Senator Nova Peris, to advance the work of the Expert Panel.[19] The committee produced reports that settled on variations to the Expert Panel's recommendations. The government also signalled its intent to announce a draft amendment to the Constitution for public consultation in late 2014.

However, other events intervened. In September 2013, most Indigenous policy and programs were moved to the Department of Prime Minister and Cabinet, and in May 2014, the Indigenous Advancement Strategy (IAS) was announced. This 'consolidated' all the items and activities that had been moved into the Prime Minister's Department and cut $534.4 million from Indigenous programs, grants and activities.[20] This occurred with limited notice to Indigenous communities whose programs and activities were overnight disestablished.

This process – and then the decisions of the IAS itself – led to a significant disempowerment of Aboriginal organisations. The notion of constitutional recognition became repugnant to those communities and organisations whose funding was cut or depleted under this new policy. The outrage accelerated a growing backlash in the community against the well-funded 'Recognise' organisation, which was prosecuting a form of constitutional recognition at odds with Aboriginal aspirations and local communities' experience. The affected communities and organisations instead saw the notion of constitutional recognition in a new light as an opportunity to address their voicelessness and powerlessness.

This backlash became so significant that Noel Pearson, Patrick Dodson, Kristie Parker (co-Chair of the National Congress of Australia's First Peoples) and Megan Davis visited Abbott to argue for another process that would enable comprehensive consultation with Aboriginal and Torres Strait Islander peoples. The Prime Minister resolved to meet with key leaders to discuss recognition. Thirty-nine leaders attended the meeting with the Prime Minister and Opposition Leader at Kirribilli in July 2015. The Aboriginal and Torres Strait Islander leaders selected to attend the summit met over the course of the weekend prior to the meeting to agree on the direction of constitutional recognition. A Statement was drafted to convey to the Prime Minister and the Opposition Leader the parameters of reform that were acceptable.

The Kirribilli Statement issued by Aboriginal and Torres Strait Islander attendees after the meeting provided:

> [A]ny reform must involve substantive changes to the Australian Constitution. It must lay the foundation for the fair treatment of Aboriginal and Torres Strait Islander peoples into the future.
>
> A minimalist approach, that provides preambular recognition, removes section 25 and moderates the race power [section 51(xxvi)], does not go far enough and would not be acceptable to Aboriginal and Torres Strait Islander peoples.[21]

The leaders also recommended that there be an ongoing dialogue between Aboriginal and Torres Strait Islander peoples and the government to negotiate the proposal to be put to referendum, as well as engagement about the acceptability of the proposed question. To undertake this, the new Prime Minister, Malcolm Turnbull, established the Referendum Council, which was jointly appointed by the Prime Minister and Leader of the Opposition Bill Shorten on 7 December 2015. The Council then commenced its work, which would lead to the Uluru Statement from the Heart. Before setting out this process, we examine the changes to the Constitution supported by the Expert Panel and other bodies.

5

WHAT DID THE EXPERT PANEL RECOMMEND?

Years of debate and effort produced a broad-ranging acceptance by Australia's political leaders that the Constitution should be changed to recognise Aboriginal and Torres Strait Islander peoples. Prime Minister John Howard adopted a preference for symbolic recognition at the 1999 referendum. This would have added new opening words to the Constitution, including: 'honouring Aborigines and Torres Strait Islanders, the nation's first people, for their deep kinship with their lands and for their ancient and continuing cultures which enrich the life of our country'.[1]

Another clause would also have been added to the Constitution to make it clear that this preamble would only be of symbolic effect. It provided that the new preamble had no legal force and could not be used in interpreting the rest of the document, or indeed any other law.

Howard's preamble was rejected by the Australian people, and so was not inserted into the Constitution. However, his idea for symbolic recognition was adopted by Australia's states. Beginning with Victoria, each state has inserted new, introductory text into their constitutions recognising Aboriginal peoples. In the case of Victoria, Queensland, New South Wales and South Australia, this has been accompanied by a clause making it clear that the new words have no legal effect.

The debate about recognition evolved beyond state-based symbolic recognition with the cross-party, Expert Panel formed by the Gillard government. The Panel decided that symbolic change must be accompanied by more substantive alterations to the Constitution. It is important to note that the Expert Panel decided the options to go out to the Australian community for consultation. The Panel featured a number of key figures and leaders in Indigenous rights over the years, including Patrick Dodson, Fred Chaney, Marcia Langton and Noel Pearson. Patrick Dodson had been a member of the Referendum Council and intimately understood the recommendations from that decade-long statutory process. Consequently, the Panel had a substantial corporate knowledge of prior recommendations for constitutional recognition, including that the Council for Aboriginal Reconciliation and the Social Justice Package had emphasised both substantive and symbolic recognition. Its January 2012 report reflected strong popular support for such changes, and the fact that Aboriginal people have for decades focused on symbolic change and substantive legal reforms.

Among other things, the Expert Panel recommended removing the remaining references to 'race' from the Constitution, inserting a new federal power to make laws with respect to Aboriginal and Torres Strait Islander peoples, and inserting a clause prohibiting racial discrimination.

The recommendations of the Expert Panel were then considered by a Joint Select Committee on Constitutional Recognition of Aboriginal and Torres Strait Islander Peoples. The Joint Select Committee set out some variations on the reform options. Otherwise, its primary conclusions were the same as that of the Expert Panel, that a successful referendum must:

- recognise Aboriginal and Torres Strait Islander peoples as the first peoples of Australia;
- preserve the Commonwealth's power to make laws with respect to Aboriginal and Torres Strait Islander peoples; and
- in making laws under such a power, prevent the Commonwealth from discriminating against Aboriginal and Torres Strait Islander peoples.[2]

Before we turn to the Uluru Statement, we describe in this chapter the ways in which the Constitution could be changed based upon the words proposed by the Expert Panel and Joint Select Committee. We examine the proposals under five categories: symbolic recognition, removing race-based clauses, inserting a new power to make laws for Aboriginal and Torres Strait Islander peoples, prohibiting racial discrimination, and other changes.

The chapter does not examine proposals that failed to receive support from the Expert Panel or Joint Select Committee. These included the idea of creating a new seventh state or reserving seats in the federal Parliament for Indigenous peoples. Neither proposal attracted significant support from Aboriginal and Torres Islander peoples or the wider community. This reflected a view that such proposals did not meet the aspirations of that community and were undesirable due to the complexity and difficulty of implementing them within Australia's constitutional structure.

Symbolic change

Prior to Uluru, each of Australia's main political parties was in broad agreement that the Constitution should provide a statement that symbolically recognises Aboriginal and Torres Strait Islander peoples. The parties accepted that this statement should acknowledge things such as the custodianship of Australia's lands and waters by Indigenous peoples and their culture and languages.

In 1999, Howard had proposed that words to this effect be included in a new preamble to the Constitution. In prefacing the Constitution as a whole, this preamble could not acknowledge Aboriginal peoples alone, as this would have made little sense as a general introduction to the document that constitutes the entire nation. Hence, Howard's draft also spoke of the 'Australian people', 'immigrants' and concepts such as 'national unity' and 'equality of opportunity for all'. Capturing the nation in this way is by its nature difficult and controversial. In 1999, it provoked questions about which peoples deserve to be referred to, and what values best express the nation's goals.

Howard's proposal for a new preamble was also awkward because the Constitution already has a preamble of sorts. This can be found at the beginning of the *Commonwealth of Australia Constitution Act 1900*, the British Act that brought the Australian Constitution into force. The preamble to that law states:

> WHEREAS the people of New South Wales, Victoria, South Australia, Queensland, and Tasmania, humbly relying on the blessing of Almighty God, have agreed to unite in

> one indissoluble Federal Commonwealth under the Crown of the United Kingdom of Great Britain and Ireland, and under the Constitution hereby established:
>
> And whereas it is expedient to provide for the admission into the Commonwealth of other Australasian Colonies and possessions of the Queen:
>
> Be it therefore enacted by the Queen's most Excellent Majesty, by and with the advice and consent of the Lords Spiritual and Temporal, and Commons, in this present Parliament assembled, and by the authority of the same, as follows ...[3]

No attempt was made in 1999 to alter this preamble to the British Act. This was because it was, and remains, unclear whether the Australian people can change these words via a referendum, or whether any such change must be made by the British Parliament. As a result, the 1999 proposal was to add a second preamble at the beginning of the Constitution, thereby giving rise to legal uncertainty about the relationship between the two.

The Expert Panel avoided this problem by suggesting that symbolic words of recognition be included as preambular language in a new section 51A in the body of the Constitution, replacing the races power. In this form, these words would serve as an introduction to the new federal power over Aboriginal affairs discussed below. The Expert Panel recommended that the following text be added:

> **Section 51A Recognition of Aboriginal and Torres Strait Islander peoples**
>
> **Recognising** that the continent and its islands now known as Australia were first occupied by Aboriginal and Torres Strait Islander peoples;
>
> **Acknowledging** the continuing relationship of Aboriginal and Torres Strait Islander peoples with their traditional lands and waters;
>
> **Respecting** the continuing cultures, languages and heritage of Aboriginal and Torres Strait Islander peoples;
>
> **Acknowledging** the need to secure the advancement of Aboriginal and Torres Strait Islander peoples.

These words would be followed by a power to make laws for 'Aboriginal and Torres Strait Islander peoples'.[4]

Public reaction focused on the use of the term 'advancement' in the final line. It was included to make it clear that the new power was to be used in a positive way. The term was chosen over other options, such as 'benefit', 'well-being' or 'free, prior and informed consent' primarily because of its legal meaning. The word 'advancement' is already used in other legal contexts, such as the *Convention on the Elimination of All Forms of Racial Discrimination* and in the preamble to the *Native Title Act 1993*. In addition, 'advancement' had a political pedigree as it was used in the early Aboriginal rights movement and was in the name of the Federal Council for the

Advancement of Aborigines and Torres Strait Islanders that led the Yes case at the 1967 referendum.

Despite this, the use of 'advancement' attracted criticism. In addition to its legal context, the term also recalled paternalistic and discriminatory state laws and policies providing for things such as Aboriginal protection and the removal of children. For this reason, some people, including some Indigenous Australians, suggested it was an inappropriate word to adopt in a recognition exercise. For example, the 2013 Youth Report on Constitutional Recognition stated: 'the term "advancement" does not adequately reflect Indigenous peoples' right to self-determination as it implies that governments can determine what is best for us'.[5]

In response to such concerns, the 2015 Joint Select Committee proposed that the final clause of section 51A referring to 'advancement' be removed. It also reopened the idea put by Howard, but rejected by the Expert Panel – on the basis that it was legally risky – that recognition occur by way of new opening words to the Constitution. It did not propose a new preamble, but instead what it termed an 'introductory statement to the Constitution'. It put forward the following, inspired by the South African Constitution, as an example of what such a statement might look like:

> We, the people of Australia:
>
> Recognising that the continent and its islands now known as Australia were first occupied by Aboriginal and Torres Strait Islander peoples;

Acknowledging the continuing relationship of Aboriginal and Torres Strait Islander peoples with their traditional lands and waters; and

Respecting the continuing cultures, languages and heritage of Aboriginal and Torres Strait Islander peoples;

Acknowledging our collective history and shared future;

Honouring those who have fought for justice and freedom;

Respecting those who have worked to build, develop and protect our country;

Commit ourselves to this Constitution.[6]

Removing race-based clauses

Australia is now the only nation in the world with a Constitution that contains a clause that empowers a national Parliament to discriminate against a group on the basis of their race. Understandably, many Australians are surprised to learn that such provisions still have a place in the Constitution. It is common to hear the view expressed that such terms were surely removed decades ago in the 1967 referendum.

This, however, did not occur. The Constitution still contains the following two sections:

25. Provision as to races disqualified from voting

For the purposes of the last section, if by the law of any State all persons of any race are disqualified from voting at elections for the more numerous House of the Parliament of the State, then, in reckoning the number of the people of the State or of the Commonwealth, persons of that race resident in that State shall not be counted.

51. Legislative powers of the Parliament

The Parliament shall, subject to this Constitution, have power to make laws for the peace, order, and good government of the Commonwealth with respect to: …

(xxvi.) The people of any race for whom it is deemed necessary to make special laws:[7]

Section 25 is expressed as a penalty. This section was modelled on the United States 14th Amendment, which aimed to discourage states from denying the vote to certain races. Section 25 operates upon section 24 of the Constitution, which provides that the House of Representatives shall be composed of members 'directly chosen by the people of the Commonwealth' and the number of seats each state has in that House 'shall be in proportion to the respective numbers of their people'.[8] Section 25 means that, if a state excludes all people of a race from voting for its lower house, that state cannot include those people in its population count that would be used to determine its representation in the federal Parliament. The section acts as a disincentive to disenfranchising people on the basis of race, but nonetheless recognises that such action is permissible.

Section 25 is known as a 'dead letter' because it is addressed to past historical circumstances that are not likely to be repeated. Its original intent was not directed at Aboriginal and Torres Strait Islander peoples. Any attempt by a state or territory to deny the vote to certain races today could fall foul of the *Racial Discrimination Act 1975*.

As we saw in chapter 2, section 51(xxvi), known as the 'races power', was altered at the 1967 referendum by deleting the words 'other than the aboriginal race in any State'. This had the effect of extending that power to Aboriginal people, for good or ill.

As the group that has most often been subjected to discrimination under the law – such as in regard to voting rights – Aboriginal people have spoken powerfully about their desire to see such clauses removed. Doing this would help modernise the Australian Constitution and bring it into line with contemporary community values.

The Expert Panel recorded overwhelming community support for deleting sections 25 and 51(xxvi). Of the submissions it received that referred to these provisions, 97.5 per cent supported the repeal of section 25, while 94 per cent supported change to the races power. Independent polling conducted by the Expert Panel of the community at large also found that 73 per cent of respondents were in favour of removing these provisions.

These findings reflect the generally held view that the concept of 'race' should not have any place in the Constitution. As Aboriginal leader Noel Pearson has argued:

> As long as the allowance of racial discrimination remains in our Constitution, it continues, in both subtle and unsubtle ways, to affect our relationships with each other. Though it has historically hurt my people more than others, racial categorisations dehumanise us all. It dehumanises us because we are each individuals, and we should be judged as individuals. We should be rewarded on our merits and assisted in our needs. Race should not matter.[9]

The concept of race found its way into the Australian Constitution because it had been widely used for much of the 19th century, including, for example, to justify the maintenance of slavery in the United States. The term was often spoken in colonial and other settings to indicate that one group of people was superior to another, and so to justify things such as unequal treatment and the denial of rights and protection to certain groups.

This differential treatment was a social and cultural construct used to justify treating groups differently. The idea that one group of people can be considered superior to another due to genetic or other differences has no scientific basis. The Expert Panel stated: 'In contemporary practice and scholarship, the dominant view among biological scientists, anthropologists and social theorists is that the concept of "race" is socially constructed, imprecise, arbitrary and incapable of definition or scientific demonstration'.[10]

Inserting a new power

The races power not only incorporates the possibility of laws that discriminate against Aboriginal and Torres Strait Islander people. Its primary function has been to support laws that benefit that group. This includes legislation recognising their interests in land in the form of native title and cultural heritage protection. The power also provides a source of authority to make direct federal payments in areas such as Indigenous education, employment and housing.

Repealing the races power could mean that such legislation and payments for Aboriginal people would become invalid and so unlawful. It would also mean that one of the key achievements of the 1967 referendum, the ability of the federal Parliament to make national laws for Aboriginal people, would be undone. As a result, it is accepted that the races power needs to be replaced, rather than repealed.

Although the races power enables the making of laws for any race, a replacement power need only deal with the making of laws for Aboriginal and Torres Strait Islander peoples – laws on the basis of culture, not race. This is because there is no other race within Australia that might conceivably be the subject of such laws. Where there are other distinct groups within the community, these are typically not defined by the concept of race but by other factors such as their nationality, culture or religion. As a result, there are no laws on the federal statute book, nor is it apparent that there have ever been, that apply the races power to groups other than Aboriginal and Torres Strait Islander peoples.

The wording of a replacement to the races power has been

the subject of considerable legal debate. One area of contention is whether it should be expressed as what is known as a 'subject matter power' or as a 'person's power'. As a subject matter power, the replacement would list a broad range of matters over which the Commonwealth can pass laws. An example of drafting of this kind provided by the Joint Select Committee would be a power to pass laws regarding:

> the cultures, languages and heritage of Aboriginal and Torres Strait Islander peoples and the relationship of Aboriginal and Torres Strait Islander peoples with their traditional lands and waters.[11]

The challenge in drafting the power this way is that it must encompass every current and future subject upon which the federal Parliament may wish to legislate for Aboriginal peoples. It is not clear that this wording does this. For example, it may not be broad enough to provide the support currently available under the races power for payments to Aboriginal people in areas such as housing or employment, or authorise the entering into of a treaty between the Commonwealth and Aboriginal peoples. Similarly, while the words would encompass laws about native title, they may not extend to new rights particular to Aboriginal people that might be identified by the High Court.

Many of these doubts could be overcome by relying on the other powers of the federal Parliament listed in section 51 of the Constitution, such as those over inter-state trade and commerce, corporations and external affairs. Where these are insufficient, the Commonwealth can seek a referral of power from the states or can channel the payment of moneys to Aboriginal people via the states. However, relying upon the states in this way runs counter to one of the primary objects of the 1967 referendum, which was to vest such power directly in the hands of the Commonwealth.

These concerns can be avoided by drafting the replacement power as a person's power. This would match the scope of the current races power in so far as it applies to Indigenous peoples. This was the approach recommended by the Expert Panel and endorsed by the Joint Select Committee. After setting out the symbolic words of recognition discussed above, the new section 51A would permit the federal Parliament to make laws 'with respect to Aboriginal and Torres Strait Islander peoples'.[12]

In this form, the power could be used by the federal Parliament to enact laws generally for and about Indigenous peoples.

As we will see in chapter 6, repealing or replacing the races power did not feature prominently in the Uluru law reform proposal agreed to during the First Nations Regional Dialogues. This was because the alternative forms of wording can never prevent racially discriminatory adverse laws. Whether it is a 'peoples' power or 'subject matter' power or whether there is a preambular statement that seeks to confine the power to beneficial laws using words such as 'advancement' or 'for the betterment', there is no iron-clad guarantee that can be made that the power cannot be used for adverse purposes. Consequently, at Uluru it was determined that for the races power, the change is no better than the status quo. As a result, Indigenous peoples did not prioritise amending or repealing the races power as a meaningful form of constitutional recognition.

Prohibiting racial discrimination

Deleting the races power and replacing it with new wording like that recommended by the Expert Panel would remove a reference to race from the Constitution. However, it would not prevent the federal Parliament from using its power to discriminate against Aboriginal and Torres Strait Islander peoples. This is because the revised wording is silent on the sorts of laws that could be passed under the power. Any law would be valid so long as it concerned Aboriginal and Torres Strait Islander peoples, whether or not it imposed negative consequences upon them or discriminated against them. As a result, like the races power, the replacement power could still be used to pass laws denying Aboriginal people the vote or prohibiting them from types of employment.

The federal Parliament has legislated to provide extensive protection from racial discrimination in the form of the *Racial Discrimination Act 1975*. For example, section 9 of that law states:

> It is unlawful for a person to do any act involving a distinction, exclusion, restriction or preference based on race, colour, descent or national or ethnic origin which has the purpose or effect of nullifying or impairing the recognition, enjoyment or exercise, on an equal footing, of any human right or fundamental freedom in the political, economic, social, cultural or any other field of public life.[13]

Section 10 of the same Act makes it clear that protection from racial discrimination applies to federal, state and territory laws. This has had a powerful impact upon state and territory laws, which, by virtue of section 109 of the Constitution, are rendered invalid where they are inconsistent with a federal law. For example, the High Court struck down a Queensland law which sought to extinguish native title because the law was inconsistent with the *Racial Discrimination Act*.[14]

While the states and territories cannot escape the effect of the *Racial Discrimination Act*, the Commonwealth can. It has the power to repeal, amend or suspend the Act, as it is one of its own laws. It did this in 1998 by suspending the operation of the Act for native title. More recently, the *Racial Discrimination Act* was suspended for the Northern Territory intervention by the *Northern Territory National Emergency Response Act 2007*.

The *Racial Discrimination Act* cannot restrict how the federal Parliament might use any new power inserted into the Constitution. The only way of negating the possibility such a power might be used to discriminate against Indigenous people is to insert qualifying words into the Constitution itself. That is why the Expert Panel recommended that the following new section be added:

Section 116A Prohibition of racial discrimination

1 The Commonwealth, a State or a Territory shall not discriminate on the grounds of race, colour or ethnic or national origin.
2 Subsection (1) does not preclude the making of laws or measures for the purpose of overcoming

> disadvantage, ameliorating the effects of past discrimination, or protecting the cultures, languages or heritage of any group.[15]

The first part of this section prohibits discrimination against any person on the listed grounds that occurs by way of laws or government actions. The second part makes it clear that this prohibition does not prevent laws or policies of a kind sometimes referred to as a 'special measure' or 'positive discrimination'. For example, the second part would preserve funding programs directed to Aboriginal people to overcome disadvantage in health or education. Similarly, it would remain possible to protect the culture, language or heritage of any group, including Aboriginal and Torres Strait Islander peoples.

This section would affect how Parliament makes laws and how the High Court considers them. At the law-making stage, Parliament would need to consider carefully whether a new law might infringe the prohibition, perhaps because it discriminates against Aboriginal people. It would have an incentive for doing so. If its law imposed discrimination of a prohibited kind, it could be struck down by the High Court. This possibility would promote greater deliberation and scrutiny of laws affecting Aboriginal people within the federal Parliament. It could act as a significant check upon a government rushing legislation through Parliament.

An example of how section 116A might operate is provided by the Northern Territory intervention. In 2007, the *Report of the Northern Territory Board of Inquiry into the Protection of Aboriginal Children from Sexual Abuse* (known as the *Little Children are Sacred* report) detailed widespread sexual abuse of

Aboriginal children. The response of the federal government led by Prime Minister John Howard was swift. The government announced a federal 'intervention' in the Northern Territory involving changes to Aboriginal land ownership, mandatory health checks for Aboriginal children, bans on the supply of alcohol and pornography in Aboriginal areas, and limitations on the payment of welfare benefits.

Five Bills were introduced into Parliament to bring about these changes. These were extraordinary laws with significant human rights ramifications designed to remedy a devastating social problem. The laws – running to 604 pages – were introduced in the House of Representatives on 7 August 2007; the first at 12.32 pm, the last at 1.47 pm. This was the first time most parliamentarians had seen the Bills. Despite this, all five were passed by the House at 9.34 pm that same day. This did not leave enough time for parliamentarians to read the Bills, let alone to debate them properly or to consult with the Aboriginal people who would be affected by the law.

The Bills were subjected to greater scrutiny in the Senate, where the government did not hold a majority. The Senate referred the legislation to the Senate Standing Committee on Legal and Constitutional Affairs on 9 August, for report by 13 August. The Committee did not recommend any substantive changes. The legislation was debated in the Senate, but ultimately passed without amendment on 16 August, nine days after the Bills were first introduced.

One of the key issues before Parliament was whether the intervention justified the suspension of the *Racial Discrimination Act*. The government believed that this suspension was necessary because the laws were specifically targeted at

Indigenous Australians and deprived them of pre-existing rights. During the limited time for debate, there was little opportunity to address this. Instead, the issue became a matter of long-running controversy after the law was enacted. Parliament has since revoked the suspension of the *Racial Discrimination Act* brought about by the intervention, and has revised the legislative scheme so that it does not differentiate between people on the basis of their race.

If a clause like section 116A had been present in the Constitution, the debate in Parliament in 2007 would likely have proceeded differently. Much more attention would have been given to the question of racial discrimination, as the possibility of a High Court challenge would have forced parliamentarians to consider the question more carefully. This deliberation, and concerns about what the High Court would do, might have led to the intervention being enacted in a different form. This might have been accompanied by consultation with the people affected by the law.

If the intervention had still been enacted in the form it was in 2007, section 116A would have enabled Aboriginal people to bring a legal challenge to the intervention. They might have argued that the suspension of the *Racial Discrimination Act* infringed the guarantee against such racial discrimination. Or, it might have been argued that specific measures in the intervention, such as restrictions on welfare benefits that only applied to Aboriginal people, were racially discriminatory and so invalid.

It cannot be said with certainty what the outcome would have been. This is because the Constitution is interpreted by the High Court, and not by governments or parliaments. Only the seven judges of that court could determine whether any part of the intervention might be struck down for inconsistency with section 116A. In effect, the judges would act as independent arbiters, thereby providing an avenue for a person to challenge any law that they believe discriminates against them on one of the prohibited grounds. The intervention would be a difficult case, in part because High Court judges would be reluctant to second-guess judgments made by Parliament about how best to address a major problem of sexual abuse. A clearer example of a law that would offend section 116A is the former ban on Aboriginal people voting in federal elections.

The views of the Indigenous community on section 116A shifted by the time of the Uluru Statement from the Heart in 2017. An important factor was the High Court decision in *Maloney v The Queen*. The Court found that a Queensland law prohibiting Indigenous people from possessing alcohol was discriminatory as it limited their right to own property. However, the Court found that this was permissible discrimination as a special measure under the *Racial Discrimination Act* because it was designed to prevent alcohol abuse and protect women and children from violence.

The *Maloney* decision suggested that the concept of racial discrimination might be a difficult basis to challenge other legislation such as the Northern Territory intervention. A key issue was the willingness of the Court to defer to Parliament on what should be regarded as special measure that can justify such discrimination.

The case featured in the Regional Dialogues of Indigenous peoples that led to the Uluru Statement. It elevated concerns that the scope of section 116A would be determined entirely by the justices of the High Court. Attendees raised the issue that a non-discrimination clause deferred decision-making to justices who may have never set foot in an Indigenous community and yet would determine what is in the best interests of Indigenous women and children. It was also thought that if justices were going to defer to democratically elected representatives as they did in *Maloney*, then section 116A did not amount to a sufficient protection of Indigenous peoples from racial discrimination.

The proposed section 116A has also attracted criticism from conservative politicians and commentators. In contrast to many Indigenous peoples, they have argued that the new section might have a broad operation, such as in regard to the Northern Territory intervention. The section has also evoked concern that it could enable the High Court to discover other human rights in the Constitution, which might then be applied to strike down laws. Such concerns were expressed by then opposition leader Tony Abbott, who responded in the media to the Expert Panel's report by warning that section 116A looked like a 'one-clause Bill of Rights'.[16] Subsequently, as Prime Minister, he repeated his concerns by saying: 'Any referendum proposal that becomes a de facto Bill of Rights is highly unlikely to succeed'.[17]

This criticism is misplaced. A single clause prohibiting racial discrimination is not any form of Bill of Rights, nor could the High Court turn it into one. It would only add another protection to the list of one-off rights already in the Constitution, such as those for freedom of religion in section 116 and trial by jury in section 80. Section 116A would be narrowly focused upon protection from racial discrimination and would say nothing about other rights such as freedom of speech or association or even discrimination on other grounds such as sex or age. Moreover, the form of protection contained in section 116A is narrower than what already exists in federal law in the form of the *Racial Discrimination Act*.

Conservative political objections to section 116A have led to the development of alternative proposals to limit the scope of a replacement for the races power. In particular, the Joint Select Committee put forward an alternative whereby the replacement to the races power would enable the making of laws for and about 'Aboriginal and Torres Strait Islander peoples, *but not so as to discriminate adversely against them*'.[18]

The words in italics fulfil a similar, but more limited, role to the proposed section 116A. Language would still be inserted into the Constitution that the High Court might apply to prevent discrimination against Aboriginal people. These words could also preserve affirmative action programs for Aboriginal people because they only prohibit the making of laws that 'discriminate adversely' against them. In addition, so long as the High Court follows the approach it has taken to similar terms used elsewhere in the Constitution, it would mean that other federal powers could not be used to discriminate adversely against Aboriginal people. It is also possible, but less certain, that the limitation would bind the federal Parliament in regard to its special power to make laws for the territories, such as the law for the Northern Territory intervention. These issues would ultimately be determined by the judges of the High Court.

One important limitation on the alternative wording is that it would only apply to laws made by the federal Parliament, and not to laws made by the states and territories. This again is a significant restriction, but its impact may be small. This is because such protection is already imposed on the states and territories by the *Racial Discrimination Act*.

The most significant limitation of the alternative option is that the protection offered against racial discrimination only applies to Aboriginal and Torres Strait Islander peoples. No protection is afforded to the rest of the community. This might perhaps be explained on the basis that the change to the Constitution is directed at recognising Indigenous peoples, and only they have been the subject of federal laws discriminating on the basis of race. On the other hand, it is generally accepted that no one should be subjected to racial discrimination, and so not granting protection to the community at large may lessen support for the referendum proposal as a whole.

The idea that the Constitution, as part of recognising Australia's first peoples, should offer every person protection from racial discrimination has attracted strong public support. Independent polling of the community conducted by the expert panel found that 80 to 90 per cent of respondents favoured amending the Constitution to insert a general guarantee against laws that discriminate on the basis of race, colour or ethnic origin.

Other changes

Other suggestions have been put forward for how the Constitution ought to be changed to recognise Aboriginal and Torres Strait Islander peoples. One is to reserve seats in the federal Parliament for Indigenous peoples. A system of this kind operates in New Zealand, which since 1867 has reserved seats in its national Parliament for Māori people. A similar change has been advocated for Australia by many Indigenous leaders and communities and has been the subject of inquiries in Queensland and in New South Wales. One of the main challenges in implementing the idea would be to develop a separate Indigenous electoral roll. Determining who would be entitled to have their name put on this roll could raise fraught questions about when a person's ancestry means they are Indigenous.

The only additional change recommended by the Expert Panel was the idea of recognising languages. Strong concern was expressed by many people about the disappearance of Aboriginal languages, and it was argued that recognition of Aboriginal people in the Constitution should also encompass this aspect of their culture. The Expert Panel said that that the following section should be added to the Constitution:

Section 127A Recognition of languages

1 The national language of the Commonwealth of Australia is English.

2 The Aboriginal and Torres Strait Islander languages are the original Australian languages, a part of our national heritage.[19]

This section had been proposed by the Cape York Institute. The Panel observed:

> Recognition of Aboriginal and Torres Strait Islander languages as part of our national heritage gives appropriate recognition to the significance of those languages, especially for Aboriginal and Torres Strait Islander Australians, but for all other Australians as well. The Panel has also concluded that the recognition of English as the national language simply acknowledges the existing and undisputed position.[20]

It is not clear what the effect of section 127A might be. Is the section merely a statement of the current state of affairs, or would it have legal effect, such as by mandating the use of English in official contexts? This uncertainty led the Joint Standing Committee to recommend that the clause not be included in any referendum.

6

THE REFERENDUM COUNCIL AND ULURU PROCESS

Indigenous leaders issued the Kirribilli Statement after meeting with the Prime Minister and Opposition Leader in July 2015. Prime Minister Malcolm Turnbull responded by establishing the Referendum Council.

The work of the Referendum Council was to advise the Prime Minister and Opposition Leader on the next steps towards a referendum. Its remit was to consult with Australians nationally, including Indigenous-led consultations, and to advise of the options for a referendum proposal, the steps for finalising that proposal and a possible timetable.

The Referendum Council's work was distinguished by the 13 First Nations Regional Dialogues. These dialogues elicited a firm response to the question asked by the federal government: what is meaningful recognition to you? And on 26 May 2017, the National Constitutional Convention revealed that all 13 Regional Dialogues had answered this question in the clearest terms: Indigenous peoples seek a constitutionally protected Voice to the Parliament. The National Convention at Uluru saw representatives from across Australia come to hear and endorse the work of the dialogues.

In this chapter we examine the process that led to the

historic meeting at Uluru, including the role of the Referendum Council and Regional Dialogues.

The Referendum Council

In 2015, Indigenous leaders were concerned that the federal government was contemplating a referendum on symbolism and minimalist constitutional housekeeping: the statement of recognition proposed by the Expert Panel, and deleting a dead letter provision in section 25 and the use of the word 'race' from the Constitution. These concerns led to a meeting between Indigenous leaders, the Prime Minister and the Leader of the Opposition at Kirribilli House in 2015. The Kirribilli leaders discussed with the two parliamentary leaders the problem with symbolic recognition and the desire of communities to have a more direct say in what form of constitutional recognition would be taken to the Australian people.

One of the problems with the Expert Panel's approach was that the members of the Panel chose the reforms that were put out to the broader community. While there were more than 3500 submissions to the Expert Panel, there was little direct engagement with communities. In seeking to exercise some control over the process, Indigenous leaders in the Kirribilli Statement called for an:

> ongoing dialogue between Aboriginal and Torres Strait Islander people (via a referendum council, steering committee or other mechanism) and the Government and Parliament, based on the significant work already completed,

> to negotiate on the content of the question to be put to referendum.[1]

They also stated under the heading 'substantive issues':

> A minimalist approach that provides preambular recognition, removes section 25 and moderates the races power (section 51(xxvi)) does not go far enough and would not be acceptable to Aboriginal and Torres Strait Islander peoples.
>
> To progress these matters, clarity from the Government and Opposition of their positions on two key issues is critical: prevention of racially discriminatory laws and the proposed advisory body. There was significant concern expressed that the Constitution as it stands enables current and future parliaments to enact discriminatory measures against Aboriginal and Torres Strait Islander peoples. Any reform option must address this concern.
>
> At this stage there are several proposals on the table that are aimed at addressing this issue. These range from a stand-alone prohibition of racial discrimination (proposed new section 116A) to a new contained power to make laws for Aboriginal and Torres Strait Islander peoples that does not extend to making adverse discriminatory laws, or a role for a new advisory body established under the Constitution.

The Kirribilli Statement is important because it sets out the framework of the reform that would emerge from the Referendum Council.

The Referendum Council comprised 15 Indigenous and non-Indigenous members. It included the former Chief Justice of the High Court of Australia Murray Gleeson, Natasha Stott Despoja, Amanda Vanstone, Stan Grant, Patricia Anderson, Noel Pearson, Megan Davis and Patrick Dodson (until he moved to the Australian Senate).

The terms of reference were:

1 Lead the process for national consultations and community engagement about constitutional recognition, including a concurrent series of Indigenous designed and led consultations.

2 Be informed by the Parliamentary Joint Select Committee on Constitutional Recognition of Aboriginal and Torres Strait Islander Peoples chaired by Mr Ken Wyatt AM MP, with Deputy Chair, Senator Nova Peris OAM. The Committee will have input into the discussion paper on various issues regarding constitutional change to help facilitate an informed community discussion.

3 Consider the recommendations of the 2012 Expert Panel on Constitutional Recognition of Indigenous Australians.

4 Report to the Prime Minister and the Leader of the Opposition on: – outcomes of national consultations and community engagement about constitutional recognition, including Indigenous designed and led

> consultations; – options for a referendum proposal, steps for finalising a proposal, and possible timing for a referendum; and – constitutional issues.[2]

The Council first met on 14 December 2015 with Prime Minister Malcolm Turnbull and the Leader of the Opposition Bill Shorten in attendance. It met on 11 subsequent occasions from 2015 to the conclusion of its work in 2017 after the Uluru Statement.

The Referendum Council in its early deliberations decided that emphasis must be placed on consultation with Indigenous communities. It decided to conduct regional meetings with Aboriginal and Torres Strait Islander peoples to ascertain their support for constitutional recognition. This reflected the understanding that the constitutional recognition process involves two parties, the party doing the recognising and the party being recognised. It is important that those 'to be recognised' participate equally in the process and that there is consensus on the model of recognition.

The Referendum Council formed an Indigenous sub-committee constituted by Aboriginal and Torres Strait Islander members of the Referendum Council. This sub-committee made decisions on the structure of the consultations, the location, the methodology and the substantive options to discuss.

One of the first concerns of the sub-committee was that 'consultation' had become a dirty word in Indigenous communities. This antagonism to 'tick a box' consultation conducted by Commonwealth and state bureaucracies had been predicted by the Aboriginal and Torres Strait Islander leaders at Kirribilli. They instead sought a 'dialogue'. This meant that a new methodology had to be developed to encourage active participation and to enable participants to feel in control of the process.

Another concern of the sub-committee was the efficacy and authority of decision-making in the dialogues. ATSIC had a traditional Western liberal model of election and representation that was based upon individuals and not culture. This led to concern that decisions were being made in ways that did not reflect Aboriginal culture, including the fact that it is a collective culture based upon the authority of elders.

Similarly, the National Congress of Australia's First Peoples that succeeded ATSIC as a representative body was a model of representation that lacked cultural authority. While there were 'chambers' that included Indigenous peak bodies and organisations, there was no chamber for First Nations.

By contrast, the post-*Mabo* native title era had seen a resurgence in communities seeking models of representation that involved their cultural grouping. For this reason, the sub-committee decided that during the dialogues, decisions needed to be made by those who had cultural authority. The sub-committee structured each dialogue so as to require 60 per cent of invitations to the dialogue as traditional owners and elders, 20 per cent local Aboriginal organisations, and 20 per cent Aboriginal individuals such as Stolen Generations, youth or grandmothers.

The invitation formula was also important because like all such processes, not every single person could take part. The sub-committee was seeking a robust sample of First Nations and community sentiment. After all, watershed statements such as the Bark Petitions, Barunga, Eva Valley, Kalkaringi, the Social

Justice Package and the Council for Aboriginal Reconciliation did not involve all First Nations peoples.

The final concern for the sub-committee was to decide the options for constitutional recognition that could be discussed within each dialogue. The Terms of Reference stated that the purpose of the Council's work was to build upon the extensive work of the Expert Panel and the 2015 Joint Select Committee on Constitutional Recognition of Aboriginal and Torres Strait Islander Peoples. This meant that five forms of recognition would be the subject of the dialogues:

1 Drafting a statement acknowledging Aboriginal and Torres Strait Islander peoples as the First Australians, and inserting it either in the Constitution or outside the Constitution, either as a preamble in a new head of power or in a statutory Declaration of Recognition.
2 Amending or deleting the 'race power' section 51(xxvi), and replacing it with a new head of power (which might contain a statement of acknowledgment as a preamble to that power) to enable the continuation of necessary laws with respect to Indigenous issues.
3 Inserting into the Constitution a prohibition against racial discrimination.
4 Providing for an Indigenous Voice to be heard by Parliament, and the right to be consulted on legislation and policy that affect Aboriginal and Torres Strait Islander peoples.
5 Agreement-making, or treaty, by way of a binding agreement negotiated between two parties: the state and First Nations. Given the significant interest in this

> topic by Aboriginal and Torres Strait Islander peoples, agreement-making was included as a substantive reform option at the First Nations Regional Dialogues and was also touched on in the broader community consultations.

The next task of the Referendum Council was to seek feedback and approval from stakeholders on the dialogues. This involved a series of national meetings. The first was held in Broome with representatives of traditional owner groups across Australia. The second was held on Thursday Island with national peak bodies covering several important sectors: legal and justice, child protection and children's rights, health, and education. The third stakeholder meeting was held in Melbourne. This meeting involved people who were not representing traditional owners but were activists in the struggle, significant national leaders, Stolen Generations groups and many others. These pre-meetings involved the Council walking each group through the process, the agenda, the materials being used, such as PowerPoint and resources, and the deliberation structure.

Finally, the Referendum Council asked the Australian Institute of Aboriginal and Torres Strait Islander Studies (AIATSIS) to manage the logistics and support delegates to attend. The AIATSIS secretariat organising the Regional Dialogues implemented the invitation formula, engaged local Aboriginal land councils to convene the dialogues, assisted the land councils in inviting delegates, and organised hotels, flights and catering. This was done so the Referendum Council could be at arm's length from the process. However, what was important was that at every step the process was Indigenous designed and Indigenous led.

The Regional Dialogues

The First Nations Regional Dialogues were convened in the following locations:

- Hobart, hosted by the Tasmanian Aboriginal Corporation (9–11 December 2016)
- Broome, hosted by the Kimberley Land Council (10–12 February 2017)
- Dubbo, hosted by the New South Wales Aboriginal Land Council (17–19 February 2017)
- Darwin, hosted by the Northern Land Council (22–24 February 2017)
- Perth, hosted by the South West Aboriginal Land and Sea Council (3–5 March 2017)
- Sydney, hosted by the New South Wales Aboriginal Land Council (10–12 March 2017)
- Melbourne, hosted by the Federation of Victorian Traditional Owners Corporation (17–19 March 2017)
- Cairns, hosted by the North Queensland Land Council (24–27 March 2017)
- Ross River, hosted by the Central Land Council (31 March – 2 April 2017)
- Adelaide, hosted by the Aboriginal Legal Rights Movement Inc (7–9 April 2017)
- Brisbane (21–23 April 2017)
- Thursday Island, hosted by Torres Shire Council and a number of Torres Strait regional organisations (5–7 May 2017).

A truncated version of the dialogue, more like an information session, was held in Canberra on 10 May 2017 and hosted by the United Ngunnawal Elders Council. Finally, the National Constitutional Convention was then held at Uluru (23–26 May 2017).

The purpose of the First Nations Regional Dialogues was to ensure that Aboriginal decision-making was at the heart of the process. This was in stark contrast to how many First Nations communities had been disenfranchised by the process to date. This change of approach meant that, while the dialogue required information sessions such as civics knowledge, history and legal education on the recognition proposals, the participants drove decision-making on priorities for reform in each region.

To ensure a robust sample of community sentiment, each dialogue was conducted in precisely the same way. This meant the agenda was the same for each. The dialogue was structured as a deliberative decision-making process that engaged participants in a discussion.

The dialogue opened with an address by Pat Anderson AO as the chair of the Referendum Council. The local leaders who led the dialogue then opened the proceedings with housekeeping and the agenda for the three days. Next, the group watched a short documentary, written by Megan Davis and produced and voiced by Rachel Perkins, which showed the lengthy history of advocacy for structural reform in Australia for Indigenous peoples. Following this, the group met together to discuss the key question: what is meaningful recognition to you in your region?

The material provided to the dialogue demonstrated that advocacy for recognition has been ongoing since the 1800s. Recognition is a legal and political term that is complex and can mean symbolic and concrete measures. Constitutional recognition can be a treaty or it can be reserved seats or it can be a Voice to Parliament or it can be a statement of recognition. These approaches differ according to the extent they are backed by the force of law. Symbolism requires no action by the state. It is a statement of fact, but it is passive and creates no rights. A substantive form of recognition like a Voice to Parliament compels the state to have First Nations peoples at the table when making decisions that affect them.

Day Two focused on the law reform proposals. Megan Davis and Rachel Perkins had produced a civics clip aimed at providing fundamental information about how the Australia legal and political system works. This included the difference between a Bill and an Act of Parliament and the difference between legislation and the Constitution. This session also included discussion on the accountability mechanisms built into the system to keep governments in check. It discussed the federal system and how the Constitution distributes power across the nation, ranging from shared powers to the exclusive power of the federal Parliament. The description of powers included the races power as amended in the historic 1967 referendum. The civics documentary also set out the role of the High Court as the ultimate interpreter of the meaning of the Constitution and how that document can be amended.

Break-out groups were then conducted, with each devoted to a single option. Then, a plenary session ventilated the reactions, ideas and criticism of each option. Following this, a second round of working groups was held, but this time the groups were cross-pollinated with people from each option. In the evening, people could discuss and debate options, and then sleep on them. The next morning, a draft record of meeting was prepared before all participants signed off on the Record of Meeting.

This Record of Meeting was not shared with the next dialogue meeting or other dialogues. One of the principles underpinning the method was to avoid groupthink. In group discussions, it is often the loudest voices in a room who are heard. This deters others from participating or expressing their views. It was important that for the purposes of free, prior and informed consent, people were able to participate freely without any particular ideology or agenda dominating. The Record of Meeting was the document that showed agreement, disagreement or tension on particular matters. It also showed the prioritisation of the reforms by the regional delegates and which reforms were viewed as an urgent priority and which were not. The Record of Meeting for each region was read out at the National Constitutional Convention.

At the conclusion of each Regional Dialogue, nominees were sought to attend the National Constitutional Convention at Uluru. In some of the dialogues, nominees were invited to address the group as to why they should attend the National Convention, and a vote was taken; in others, names were placed on a board or wall. Ten delegates were chosen to represent their region. This process of identifying delegates allowed the cultural authority that had been highlighted through the dialogue process to continue at the Uluru National Convention. The continuity of knowledge was also critical.

The National Constitutional Convention was not a decision-making forum. Its purpose was to share the regional Records of Meetings, collate the reforms prioritised in each region, and settle on a single reform or reforms for constitutional recognition based on what dialogue participants had agreed to. The Referendum Council put it this way:

> The National Convention did not reopen the work that had been done in the Dialogues. Rather, the task of the National Convention was to bring together the outcomes from the Dialogues in order to arrive at a consensus.

The convenors and working group leaders from the dialogues also attended the National Convention, which took the total participants at the National Convention to 17 people from each region. The Referendum Council also invited other people, such as the Social Justice Commissioner, to attend the National Constitutional Convention to ensure a range of views were presented.

The National Constitutional Convention

The National Convention was held on 23–26 May 2017 at Yulara and Mutitjulu, near Uluru. Around 250 delegates attended from around Australia. At the opening ceremony, held at Mutitjulu, people from Arnhem Land and the Torres Strait, and Anangu men, the traditional owners of the land that the Convention was to meet on, performed three ceremonial dances. Over the next three days, delegates read out the Records of Meetings, conducted working groups on the key reforms and workshopped the way forward to a referendum.

The Convention endorsed the work of the dialogues. Although post-Uluru reporting suggests that there were votes on reforms and other such things, Uluru was only an endorsement meeting. The purpose of the national meeting was to hear the findings of each of the dialogues and to see where the results of the dialogues showed a clear consensus.

The Regional Dialogues ranked a Voice to Parliament as the first reform priority. The table overleaf shows the preferences recorded in the Records of Meeting from each dialogue. Although not on the agenda put before the dialogues, truth-telling also emerged with unanimous support at every dialogue.

Many of the proposals suggested by the Expert Panel did not feature prominently in the Regional Dialogue priorities, even though they were central to discussions.

The Regional Dialogues regarded Section 25 as a dead letter. Its removal would be highly symbolic but without substantive benefit for Aboriginal and Torres Strait Islander peoples. The fact it was not prioritised is testament to the general approach of the dialogues, which was to not clutter a referendum with excessive amounts of symbolism. Participants were determined to settle on reform that would change lives.

This sentiment influenced decision-making on the races power. The multiple approaches to the races power were all ranked low or rejected in the dialogues. This was later lamented by federal Parliament's Joint Select Committee on Constitutional Recognition of Aboriginal and Torres Strait Islander Peoples. However, the conversation in the dialogues was that if no one could provide them with a rock-solid

Reform priorities resulting from the Regional Dialogues

	Acknowledgment	Head of Power	Prohibition on Racial Discrimination	A Voice to Parliament	Agreement-making
Hobart	Not endorsed	Endorsed	Endorsed	Endorsed	Endorsed
Broome	Inconclusive	Endorsed	Not recorded	Endorsed	Not recorded
Dubbo	Not endorsed	Inconclusive	Not recorded	Endorsed	Endorsed
Darwin	Not endorsed	Inconclusive	Endorsed	Endorsed	Endorsed
Perth	Not endorsed	Endorsed	Endorsed	Endorsed	Endorsed
Sydney	Inconclusive	Inconclusive	Endorsed	Endorsed	Endorsed
Melbourne	Not endorsed	Not recorded	Not recorded	Endorsed	Endorsed
Cairns	Inconclusive	Inconclusive	Not recorded	Endorsed	Endorsed
Ross River	Endorsed	Inconclusive	Endorsed	Endorsed	Endorsed
Adelaide	Inconclusive	Inconclusive	Not recorded	Endorsed	Endorsed
Brisbane	Inconclusive	Not endorsed	Endorsed	Endorsed	Endorsed
Thursday Island	Not endorsed	Inconclusive	Endorsed	Endorsed	Endorsed
Canberra	Not endorsed	Not recorded	Not recorded	Not recorded	Not recorded

Key:

Not endorsed

Endorsed

Inconclusive

Not recorded

guarantee that an amended section 51(xxvi) or a section 51A could stop adverse discriminatory legislation, the change was the same as the status quo. Removing the word 'race' and inserting 'Aboriginal and Torres Strait Islander Peoples' would not change the possibility that Parliament would pass legislation that discriminated against Indigenous peoples. Participants at the dialogues were also alarmed that altering or deleting section 51(xxvi) could undermine beneficial legislation, particularly the *Native Title Act*.

The Referendum Council extrapolated guiding principles from the dialogues to assist discussion of reforms at the National Convention at Uluru and to frame negotiations with the government following Uluru. The guiding principles enabled the reforms to be assessed according to fundamental values expressed by the dialogues.

In coming to these principles, the Council looked to historical statements of aspirations by Aboriginal and Torres Strait Islander peoples – including the Bark Petitions of 1963, the Barunga Statement of 1988, the Eva Valley Statement of 1993, the Kalkaringi Statement of 1998, the report on the Social Justice Package by ATSIC in 1995 and the Kirribilli Statement of 2015, as well as the United Nations Declaration on the Rights of Indigenous Peoples.

The principles were that a reform proposal could only succeed at Uluru if it:

- Does not diminish Aboriginal sovereignty and Torres Strait Islander sovereignty.
- Involves substantive, structural reform.

- Advances self-determination and the standards established under the United Nations Declaration on the Rights of Indigenous Peoples.
- Recognises the status and rights of First Nations.
- Tells the truth of history.
- Does not foreclose on future advancement.
- Does not waste the opportunity of reform.
- Provides a mechanism for First Nations agreement-making.
- Has the support of First Nations.
- Does not interfere with positive legal arrangements.[3]

A handful of delegates left the Convention because they preferred a treaty to constitutional reform. One of these delegates, Lidia Thorpe (who, in 2020, became a Senator for the Greens Party), said:

> We as sovereign First Nations people reject constitutional recognition. We do not recognise occupying power or their sovereignty, because it serves to disempower, and takes away our voice ... We demand a sovereign treaty with an independent sovereign treaty commission, and appropriate funds allocated.[4]

The more than 200 other delegates endorsed and respected the work of the Regional Dialogues, and drafted and adopted the Uluru Statement from the Heart.

The consensus that emerged at Uluru was for a sequenced reform process known as 'Voice, Treaty, Truth'. We examine these reforms in the next chapter. At the end of the Convention, on 26 May 2017, Megan Davis read out the Uluru Statement from the Heart, which is set out in full in an appendix to this book. It was addressed by the delegates to the Australian people, not Australian politicians. This was decided after much deliberation, the delegates believing that too many such processes resulted in Aboriginal and Torres Strait Islander peoples handing over a statement or petition or declaration to the Australian government, often in the form of a painting on bark or other material, that is then taken back to Canberra to hang on the walls of Parliament House.

Instead, it was decided to ask the Australian people to 'walk with us in a movement of the Australian people for a better future'. This was because the Constitution can be changed by Australians. It happened in 1967. And like 1967, Aboriginal and Torres Strait Islander peoples felt that Indigenous people and the wider Australian community could work together again to change the nation. The Uluru Statement provides the logic for the reform. Delegates felt convinced that if Australians read the Uluru Statement, they would understand the urgency of the task and would support change at the ballot box to benefit the entire nation.

Consultation of the broader community

In addition to the Regional Dialogues and the National Constitutional Convention, the Referendum Council solicited the views of all Australians. This happened through online consultation, telephone survey participation and written submissions.

The online consultation examined each of the five key options. There was a brief animated video to explain the five options, and the reasoning behind and possible limitations of each option. There were also infographics, social media posts and short textual descriptions on the Council website.

Through the online mechanisms, 195 831 people actively engaged in the discussion.[5] In addition, 5300 people participated in online and telephone surveys conducted between November 2016 and May 2017. This included two samples of 2500 Australians representative of Australia's diverse geography and demography, as well as 100 Australians identifying as Aboriginal and/or Torres Strait Islander.

The Council also called for public submissions, based on a discussion paper. These were received between December 2016 and May 2017. A total of 1111 submissions were received, including 1057 submissions via an online form (structured submissions) and 54 submissions taking the form of an email, letter or other document (free-form submissions). Analysis of the submissions showed that there was strong support for recognition.

- A large majority of submissions supported all five of the key proposals.
- 93 per cent backed the inclusion of an Indigenous voice when Parliament and government make laws and policies about Indigenous affairs.
    - 77 per cent supported the creation of a group providing this voice under the Constitution.
- 91 per cent supported a statement of acknowledgment of Aboriginal and Torres Strait Islander peoples as the First Peoples of Australia.

  - 86 per cent in favour of a statement within the Constitution, and
  - 5 per cent in favour of a statement in normal Australian law.
- 85 per cent of submissions supported the removal of section 25.
- 67 per cent supported the removal of the word 'race' from the Constitution.
- 78 per cent supported the insertion of a constitutional prohibition against racial discrimination.

Report of the Referendum Council

After the Uluru National Convention and the process of public consultation had concluded, the Referendum Council handed down its final report on 30 June 2017. The report reflected the strengths of the dialogue process and the clarity that this produced. It stated:

> The integrity of the process is evidenced in the fact that the exhaustive deliberations and informed participation of participants in the First Nations Regional Dialogues led to consensus at Uluru. The outcome captured in the Uluru Statement from the Heart was a testament to the efficacy of the structured process, which allowed the wisdom and intent of the representatives of the First Nations Regional Dialogues to coalesce in a common position.[6]

The First Nations Regional Dialogues placed Indigenous peoples at the forefront of the process. This was the opposite of how the Australian Constitution had been drafted. The Referendum Council explained it in this way:

> This process is unprecedented in our nation's history and is the first time a constitutional convention has been convened with and for First Peoples. The Dialogues engaged 1200 Aboriginal and Torres Strait Islander delegates – an average of 100 delegates from each Dialogue – out of a population of approximately 600,000 people nationally. This is the most proportionately significant consultation process that has ever been undertaken with First Peoples. Indeed, it engaged a greater proportion of the relevant population than the constitutional convention debates of the 1800s, from which First Peoples were excluded.[7]

The Council endorsed the statement at Uluru and the call for Voice, Treaty, Truth. It concluded:

> In consequence of the First Nations Regional Dialogues, the Council is of the view that the only option for a referendum proposal that accords with the wishes of Aboriginal and Torres Strait Islander Peoples is that which has been described as providing, in the Constitution, for a Voice to Parliament.
>
> In principle, the establishment by the Constitution of a body to be a Voice for First Peoples, with the structure and functions of the body to be defined by Parliament,

> may be seen as an appropriate form of recognition, of both substantive and symbolic value, of the unique place of Aboriginal and Torres Strait Islander peoples in Australian history and in contemporary Australian society.[8]

The report of the Referendum Council reached this conclusion in light of how Australia's First Nations decided they should be recognised in the Constitution. It was the only option that received unanimous support in the dialogue process and so was the only possibility for constitutional recognition put forward by the Council.

The process undertaken by the Referendum Council was very different from that undertaken by the Expert Panel, and so a different result emerged. While the Expert Panel chose the options for reform and then consulted, the reform agenda produced at Uluru was the result of a ground-up, deliberative decision-making process involving 13 Regional Dialogues conducted around Australia. This provided clarity and certainty about a singular option for reform that for the first time had the backing of Indigenous peoples. The process was also underpinned by cultural authority, particularly from the traditional owners involved in the Regional Dialogue process. These factors underpinned the Referendum Council recommendation that the Voice be put to the people as a constitutional referendum.

The Referendum Council also recommended other non-constitutional changes that emerged from the Uluru Statement. These were an extra-constitutional statement of recognition, the establishment of a Makarrata commission to supervise agreement-making, and a process for truth-telling.

The Council noted that these proposed reforms were modest and substantive, reasonable, unifying and capable of attracting the necessary support from both people and politicians.

7

VOICE, MAKARRATA COMMISSION AND TRUTH

The Uluru Statement from the Heart called for a constitutionally protected Voice to Parliament, Treaty, Truth. The reforms are listed in a sequence. The sequence is deliberate, and understanding the order is central to the message of the Uluru Statement. It was based upon recognition that public institutions, politicians and political parties rarely listen to what Indigenous peoples say about their lives and aspirations. Too often these bodies rewrite, reinterpret and rearrange the things that First Peoples themselves say on matters of reform.

The sequence: Voice, then Treaty and Truth

The process was predicated on an amendment to the text of the Australian Constitution through a referendum of the Australian people. The Voice to Parliament is that reform. A treaty does not require constitutional amendment, nor does 'truth-telling', at least the way treaty and truth were contemplated by those involved in the dialogues.

The Voice to Parliament is a structural reform. It is a change to the structure of Australia's public institutions and would redistribute public power via the Constitution, Australia's highest law. The reform will create an institutional relationship between governments and First Nations that will compel the state to listen to Aboriginal and Torres Strait Islander Peoples in policy- and decision-making.

The next phase of the sequence of the Uluru reforms is a Makarrata, a process of agreement-making and truth-telling. Treaty has been a long-time aspiration for Aboriginal people. Negotiating a treaty is a nation-to-nation process and requires leverage and resources. Having a Voice to Parliament will increase the likelihood that treaty negotiations will be productive and successful.

The Voice will be an enabling mechanism for First Nations people in any treaty negotiations. Aboriginal and Torres Strait Islander peoples are, unfortunately, in a poor negotiating position compared to the state. The Voice will create the Commission that will support First Nations in those negotiations. Without the Voice, a treaty is vulnerable because of the considerable legal power of the Commonwealth. State treaty processes are particularly vulnerable, including those that are ongoing in Australia. Each runs the risk of being undermined by the Commonwealth.

Voice to Parliament

The First Nations Regional Dialogues unanimously ranked a Voice to the Australian Parliament as the number one priority in their region and for constitutional recognition. The idea of a Voice to Parliament stems from the experience of many Indigenous peoples globally who seek to find pragmatic and functional ways of influencing government. After all, many

Indigenous peoples are vulnerable to the state, whose laws and policies often shape the way their lives are lived.

Democracies also function in a way that centres elections as the primary method by which community sentiment is determined. And the ballot box, based upon free and fair periodic elections, is a numbers game, given that the representative with the greatest number of votes wins the opportunity to represent the community. The numbers game of elections plays against Indigenous peoples' issues. Aboriginal and Torres Strait Islander peoples may be the 'First Peoples', but they are less than 3 per cent of the Australian population. Majority vote at the ballot box and in Parliament means it is difficult for their voice to be heard and for them to influence laws that are made about them. It is not surprising, then, that Indigenous peoples have argued for political representation and fairer consultation for more than a century.

In 2007, the United Nations General Assembly adopted a framework of Indigenous peoples' rights that reflected global agreement on the minimum standards that should be afforded by the state. In 2009, Australia endorsed the United Nations Declaration on the Rights of Indigenous Peoples, which emphasises the importance of genuine Indigenous participation and consultation in political decisions made about their rights. However, no formal processes for this to occur have yet been implemented in Australia.

The United Nations Declaration on the Rights of Indigenous Peoples sets out treaties and agreements as separate to the kind of constitutional power envisaged by the Voice. Treaties, agreements and other constructive arrangements are critical for the state and Indigenous peoples to negotiate partnership and rights. These may be recognised constitutionally, legislatively or by way of private law in contract. However, they are separate and in addition to the kind of structural power enabled by constitutional recognition for the Voice.

While a treaty might contemplate issues that are exclusively for First Nations to lead on, the reality is that most matters will have some input from different levels of government. The idea behind a Voice to Parliament is that Aboriginal and Torres Strait Islander peoples are engaged in the development and implementation of laws, policies and programs that always affect them and their rights. This is the only way to achieve better quality policies and laws and a fairer relationship with government. This is one of the compelling reasons the First Nations dialogues thought the Constitution should be amended by establishing an Indigenous body – as many other countries have – to advise Parliament on laws and policies relating to Indigenous affairs. Such a body would ensure that the views of First Peoples are heard by lawmakers and could help Parliament enact better and more effective laws.

Other countries with a similar structure include Norway, Sweden and Finland, which all have a First Nations Parliament with various degrees of authority over some matters and a right to be consulted on legislation. In New Zealand, there are seven seats reserved in Parliament for Māori people. In Colombia, there is a constitutional provision that requires government to consult with Indigenous peoples before allowing natural resource exploitation on Indigenous lands. These examples, and the proposed Voice in Australia, are all consistent with the United Nations Declaration on the Rights of Indigenous Peoples, particularly Article 18, which states that 'Indigenous peoples have the right to participate in decision-making in matters which would affect their rights, through representatives chosen by themselves in accordance with their own procedures, as well as to maintain and develop their own indigenous decision-making institutions'.

The First Nations dialogues also discussed how a structural change of this form could prevent Parliament passing discriminatory laws and policies. If the race power in section 51(xxvi) of the Constitution were to be replaced or amended, Aboriginal people and Torres Strait Islanders would need some assurance that any new or amended power could only be used positively or for their advancement or benefit. The use of the Voice to address the concerns of Indigenous peoples about possible discriminatory legislation being passed by the federal Parliament was a solution devised in the dialogues.

This is how the Voice emerged as a preferred option to section 116A, the non-discrimination clause recommended by the Expert Panel. Section 116A was ranked high in the prioritisation of options by the First Nations regional dialogues. However, section 116A was more passive than the Voice because it could only be used when and if the government passed racially discriminatory laws. This meant that section 116A would not empower people to be actively involved upfront in the political process. Section 116A was more of a shield than a sword. If the federal Parliament passed a discriminatory law, litigation would be required to test the law, which would involve considerable financial outlay for communities and emotional costs associated with the lengthy wait and uncertainty. The Voice was considered a more effective institution to empower Indigenous communities and provide a check on Parliament.

The idea that a Voice could scrutinise or monitor the Commonwealth's use of power as it relates to Indigenous peoples is not new in Australia's constitutional system. There are many mechanisms that inform and advise the federal Parliament on such matters. The Productivity Commission, the Australian Law Reform Commission, the Auditor-General and the Australian National Audit Office are examples. Another example of such monitoring work is the scrutiny of proposed laws under the *Human Rights (Parliamentary Scrutiny) Act 2011* (Cth). All of these mechanisms are intended to improve the quality of law- and policy-making by the Commonwealth. As constitutional law professor Anne Twomey has said:

> It is hard to imagine that anyone would argue that it is better for Parliament to be ignorant and ill-informed, its laws ineffective and its expenditure wasteful. There can be no harm in listening to the views of others and using them to improve outcomes.[1]

The proposal for a Voice emerged with great enthusiasm and wide support in response to the vacuum of political representation for an Indigenous peoples that had emerged after the abolition of ATSIC. In the 2014 HC 'Nugget' Coombs oration, Marion Scrymgour, a former ATSIC Commissioner, spoke about a special advisory body made up of Indigenous representatives that would have input into government decisions affecting Aboriginal people. The idea of a constitutional advisory function or a duty to consult was also foreshadowed in the Kirribilli Statement as a possible option for a constitutional advisory body.

In 2015, a federal parliamentary committee added a constitutional advisory function to its list of alternative forms of constitutional recognition outside of the Expert Panel recommendations. That committee had the benefit of substantive submissions from the Cape York Institute, which had spent half a decade developing the proposal, including studying the Waitangi Tribunal and Māori legal and political recognition, as well as the Sami Parliaments in Finland, Norway and Sweden. This reflected the view of Aboriginal lawyer Noel Pearson that effective recognition meant giving Indigenous peoples a better say in the democratic processes affecting their affairs.

Such reforms have been frequently suggested over the years. The Barunga Statement in 1988 called for 'A national elected Aboriginal and Islander organisation to oversee Aboriginal and Islander affairs'. The Barunga Statement also called for 'the Commonwealth Parliament to negotiate with us a Treaty recognising our prior ownership, continued occupation and sovereignty and affirming our human rights and freedom'.

The calls for reform over the past century show that there is an advocacy for a voice within the democratic framework of the state as a pragmatic way of First Nations adapting to the imposed legal and political environment. There is also advocacy for a framework for a treaty that would enable communities to practise self-determination. This two-tier approach is common in countries with significant Indigenous populations to ensure every possible mechanism can be adopted to influence the state and to leverage public power to drive change in communities.

The idea of enshrinement or constitutional protection of the Voice is key to the capacity of communities to drive change.

Each First Nations dialogue spoke to the need for this Voice to be durable and sustainable and so to exist beyond any one political cycle. Many lamented the fact that Indigenous affairs was a 'political football' and that Indigenous issues are subject to political whim. Communities saw the ideological nature of Indigenous affairs as being one reason why there is so much entrenched disadvantage.

Some First Nations dialogue participants spoke about the business, pastoralist and farmer demands for 'certainty' after the *Mabo* decision by the High Court of Australia, and said this applies equally to Indigenous affairs. They felt that they should equally have some certainty from one political cycle to the next about their funding and programs. This would enable communities to plan for the future and strategise for a longer term beyond the three-year period between federal elections.

The Referendum Council report made its recommendation for the Voice in the following terms:

> That a referendum be held to provide in the Australian Constitution for a representative body that gives Aboriginal and Torres Strait Islander First Nations a Voice to the Commonwealth Parliament. One of the specific functions of such a body, to be set out in legislation outside the Constitution, should include the function of monitoring the use of the heads of power in section 51(xxvi) and section 122 [the territories power]. The body will recognise the status of Aboriginal and Torres Strait Islander Peoples as the First Peoples of Australia.[2]

The Referendum Council recommended that the Constitution be amended to create a Voice to Parliament. It did not recommend enshrining an entire model. Instead, the detail would be deferred to Parliament. Getting the balance right is challenging. Too little detail may not be sufficient for an informed vote, while too much detail may be problematic in not leaving flexibility for Parliament to decide how the Voice will work and to adapt this over time.

One approach identified by the Referendum Council is to hold the referendum first and design the Voice later. Another approach is to design it first so people have a model in mind that Parliament might enact after the referendum. This could help Australians make a more informed decision at the ballot box and allay concerns about what the Voice might look like.

The idea of leaving the design of an institution later to Parliament was used by the Australian drafters of the Constitution when they created the High Court of Australia. They enshrined the Court in the Constitution, and it was designed and passed in legislation a few years later. Referendums are the same. The rules in section 128 set up the referendum and defers detail on the referendum to Parliament. This is consistent with what former High Court Chief Justice Murray Gleeson has said about the design of the Voice:

> The structure, composition and functions of [the Voice] would be determined, and susceptible to change, by legislation of the Federal Parliament. What would appear in the Constitution would be the minimum requirements necessary to guarantee its continued existence and its essential characteristics.[3]

Within this framework, some aspects of the design of the Voice were still put forward. The Referendum Council Final Report said that the Voice must:

> have authority from, be representative of, and have legitimacy in Aboriginal and Torres Strait Islander communities across Australia. It must represent communities in remote, rural and urban areas, and not be comprised of handpicked leaders. The body must be structured in a way that respects culture. Any body must also be supported by a sufficient and guaranteed budget, with access to its own independent secretariat, experts and lawyers. It was also suggested that the body could represent Aboriginal and Torres Strait Islander Peoples internationally. A number of Dialogues said the body's representation could be drawn from an Assembly of First Nations, which could be established through a series of treaties among nations.[4]

The Voice as envisaged by many dialogues would be First Nations based, not individual based. First Nations based means that the electorates would be drawn from the collectives of Aboriginal nations country-wide. The collective is the way Aboriginal culture exists. The people eligible would likely be the body of traditional owners, which means that members of the Voice represent their cultural authority. This would render the decision-making of the Voice very serious and deeply embedded in communities. One thing each dialogue had said was that the sector peak bodies who do service delivery in communities are not representative of communities and are not their voice. There was some tension about how these bodies purport to represent community sentiment to politicians in Canberra but never report back. This means there is very little accountability.

The dialogues proposed that the First Nations themselves would determine how they are represented. This would occur in line with their right to self-determination via a further national dialogue process that allowed them to drive design (rather than merely consultation on a pre-designed model).

On the question of representation, all groups said the model must be First Nations based, but some groups in dialogues expressed a commitment to liberal democratic governance and said that the selection of a cultural authority among a group should be conducted by ballot box elections. This would mean engaging, as did ATSIC and the National Congress of Australia's First Peoples, the Australian Electoral Commission to supervise elections. Other First Nations could immediately identify who had the cultural authority to represent them. Others might seek to retain existing mechanisms of statutory land rights or native title such as prescribed body corporates. Concerns about manageable numbers saw other First Nations contemplate cultural authority via regional groupings.

Where conversations turned to how many people might make up the Voice, some said 200 representatives in an Assembly and some said 72. Either way, it was agreed that institutional design should not be led by the question: what is the right number for the Voice to be manageable? They felt that this question serves bureaucrats and governments who seek a manageable number for their own processes. They pointed to governments relying upon a few unrepresentative leaders in the absence of ATSIC's 32 representatives and 12-member national board.

It was clear during the dialogues that Indigenous grassroots communities felt disempowered and voiceless and did not believe that the many structures and groups that surround them are representing their thoughts and needs and wants. This also reflected poor outcomes from political leaders and bureaucracies. There was a very clear aspiration to have a direct connection between Canberra and community. There was little appetite for generalist elections, whereby those with sophisticated Western-style résumés are more appealing than those without. ATSIC was spoken of as having had a regional governance model that worked well because it was drawn from people who lived in communities and regions, not capital cities. It was felt that the Voice could follow this path to accommodate the diverse ways in which First Nations express their cultural authority and legitimacy.

It was felt that to achieve this the Voice must be entrenched in the Constitution. Doing so would ensure that the Voice is not subject to easy repeal by Parliament. The Referendum Council noted that a constitutionally entrenched Voice was important to participants in the Regional Dialogues and the National Convention

> because of the history of poor or nonexistent consultation with communities by the Commonwealth. Consultation is either very superficial or it is more meaningful, but then wholly ignored.
>
> For Dialogue participants, the logic of a constitutionally enshrined Voice – rather than a legislative body alone – is that it provides reassurance and recognition that this new

norm of participation and consultation would be different to the practices of the past.[5]

Treaty

The second reform called for in the First Nations Regional Dialogues was a Makarrata Commission to oversee a process of agreement-making and truth-telling. As we saw in chapter 3, the Yolngu word Makarrata ('the coming together after a struggle' or 'things are all right again after a conflict') was adopted by the treaty campaign in the 1970s. The term 'agreement-making' is interchangeable with 'treaty'. It means a binding agreement between a First Nation and the state that has legal effect and is aimed at resolving difficult problems by negotiation rather than fighting things out in court or governments imposing top-down legislation.

Treaty, or agreement-making, has been an ambition of many Aboriginal and Torres Strait Islander people for decades. However, federal governments have mostly ignored this call. There was some interest in a treaty under the government of Prime Minister Malcolm Fraser, and Bob Hawke committed to a treaty as Prime Minister. This became a broken promise. At the time of the Referendum Council's work, Victoria and South Australia were actively pursuing treaty agreements. However, such processes depend upon the government of the day and its political priorities. South Australia had a treaty process under a Labor government, but once that government lost office, the treaty process was abandoned.

Pursuing a treaty or treaties was strongly supported in the dialogues and at the National Convention because this course of action has always been viewed as an important path to reconciliation. The dialogues in the official record of discussion described it in this way:

> there is Unfinished Business to resolve. And the way to address these differences is through agreement-making.
>
> > 'Treaty was seen as the best form of establishing an honest relationship with government.' (Dubbo)
>
> Makarrata is another word for Treaty or agreement-making. It is the culmination of our agenda. It captures our aspirations for a fair and honest relationship with government and a better future for our children based on justice and self-determination.
>
> > 'If the community can't self-determine and make decisions for our own community regarding economic and social development, then we can't be confident about the future for our children.' (Wreck Bay)
>
> Through negotiated settlement, First Nations can build their cultural strength, reclaim control and make practical changes over the things that matter in their daily life. By making agreements at the highest level, the negotiation process with the Australian government allows First Nations to express our sovereignty – the sovereignty that we know comes from The Law.[6]

It was recognised at the Regional Dialogues that for a treaty process to occur, the community needs considerably more resources to engage with the state, as well as a lengthy period for planning. A number of dialogues referred to the Waitangi Tribunal in New Zealand as an example of how an institutional body could assist communities in preparing to negotiate agreements.

Many dialogues expressed hurt at the native title process and how it has torn communities apart and inflamed intracultural disputes and tensions. For this reason, many dialogues said that there needed to be a treaty 'with ourselves' or among each other in order to learn how to work together again.

Those who had participated in the native title system spoke about how disenfranchised they felt with that system. They said that the courts, native title services bodies and land councils that are ostensibly set up to protect and service Indigenous communities often fail to do so. Native title groups are under-resourced and are required to enter into agreements such as Indigenous Land Use Agreements where there is often a serious power imbalance. The sector attracts lawyers and other parties who can take advantage of impecunious communities at sea in a complex regulatory system. They also expressed concern that the native title system, if not the entire ecosystem of Indigenous affairs, forces communities to 'incorporate' their affairs by creating a company structure. Much was said about the incongruous nature of Western-style incorporation and that communities become bogged down in procedural matters, such as minutes and board elections, and less time is spent on strategic and unifying activities that bring communities together. Both the *Corporations (Aboriginal and Torres Strait Islander) Act 2006* (Cth) and the *Corporations Act 2001* (Cth), and accompanying regulators, were singled out for criticism in virtually all dialogues.

It is important to note that not all dialogues ranked Treaty highly. In the Broome dialogue, for example, many people expressed fatigue with agreement-making because so much of this was conducted once strong native title claims have been successful and recognised. The importance of the dialogues process is that it elicited a complex and nuanced picture of communities across Australia. No one community is like another and no one person or group can speak for all communities. This showed the power of the dialogues in avoiding groupthink or pre-existing political agendas.

Truth

The final aspect of the sequence was truth-telling. During the dialogues, each region sought to speak first about their history and its place in the nation's story before they wanted to speak about the Constitution. Many made the point that you cannot recognise that which you do not know. Although truth-telling was not an option for reform that was put to the dialogues, it was clear to the Referendum Council that there was a desire in each community for there to be more emphasis on truth-telling.

The need for people to know more about Australian and Aboriginal history was repeatedly raised in the dialogues. Across Australia, the idea of history and truth-telling emerged as a strong theme. This led the Referendum Council to capture the richness in 'Our Story', the Aboriginal history of Australia that follows the one-page Uluru Statement from the Heart. This story commences:

> Our First Nations are extraordinarily diverse cultures, living in an astounding array of environments, multi-lingual across many hundreds of languages and dialects. The continent was occupied by our people and the footprints of our ancestors traversed the entire landscape. Our songlines covered vast distances, uniting peoples in shared stories and religion. The entire land and seascape is named, and the cultural memory of our old people is written there. This rich diversity of our origins was eventually ruptured by colonisation. Violent dispossession and the struggle to survive a relentless inhumanity has marked our common history. The First Nations Regional Dialogues on constitutional reform bore witness to our shared stories.

The truth-telling ventilated by 13 Regional Dialogues involved many facets of Australian history from Captain Cook to the brute force of the Protection Era and on to land rights and activism. On Captain Cook and the Australia story of nation, 'Our Story' says:

> Australia was not a settlement and it was not a discovery. It was an invasion.
>
>> 'Cook did not discover us, because we saw him. We were telling each other with smoke, yet in his diary, he said "discovered".' (Torres Strait Regional Dialogue)

> 'Australia must acknowledge its history, its true history. Not Captain Cook. What happened all across Australia: the massacres and the wars. If that were taught in schools, we might have one nation, where we are all together.' (Darwin Regional Dialogue)
>
> The invasion that started at Botany Bay is the origin of the fundamental grievance between the old and new Australians: that Australia was colonised without the consent of its rightful owners.
>
> Now is an opportunity for the First Nations to tell the truth about history in our own voices and from our own point of view.
>
> And for mainstream Australians to hear those voices and to reconsider what they know and understand about their nation's history. This will be challenging, but the truth about invasion needs to be told.

Many dialogues then discussed how truth-telling had been conducted in Australian legal and political contexts. Over the last 30 years, several important truth-telling processes have been carried out in Australia, particularly in commissions and reports, including the Royal Commission into Aboriginal Deaths in Custody, the *Bringing Them Home* report on the Stolen Generations, the Australian Law Reform Commission report into recognition of Aboriginal customary law and the Council for Aboriginal Reconciliation's final report. These show the many ways the state has asked Indigenous peoples to tell their stories to understand the truth of history to avoid repeating the wrongs of the past. Despite this, Australia's understanding of colonial history, the dispossession and the genocide, the Frontier Wars and massacres, and discriminatory policies are not well understood. One quote from the Ross River dialogue demonstrates the importance of truth-telling:

> Participants expressed disgust about a statue of John McDouall Stuart being erected in Alice Springs following the 150th anniversary of his successful attempt to reach the Top End. This expedition led to the opening up of the 'South Australian frontier' which lead to massacres as the telegraph line was established and white settlers moved into the region. People feel sad whenever they see the statue; its presence and the fact that Stuart is holding a gun is disrespectful to the Aboriginal community who are descendants of the families slaughtered during the massacres throughout central Australia.[7]

Overall, the dialogues were overwhelmingly of the view that a nation cannot recognise people they do not know or understand.

Having said that, there was also a pragmatic view about the way power works in Canberra. Many were exhausted by the endless calls for Aboriginal people to give voice to truth-telling and their version of history. They also felt that this never alters or penetrates the national narrative and so viewed truth-telling as a way of delaying or avoiding the recognition of substantive and concrete rights. Many alluded to Prime Minister Bob Hawke's failed promise for a treaty and national land rights. When he did not deliver on treaty, he instead set up a statutory process for reconciliation so that Australians could get to know Aboriginal and Torres Strait Islander peoples better.

In light of this history, the dialogues did not demand a truth-telling process or a truth commission. They also did not want the opportunity of constitutional power through the Voice communities to be given up in favour of another truth-telling process that could drain people of their emotional energy and for which there would be no end in sight.

There was a strong view that truth-telling is being done now but it needs more coordination. Statutory land rights and native title require First Nations people to collate their histories and stories. Many First Nations people do this on a daily basis with high schools, community groups, businesses and local historical societies. Many communities are also actively involved with local councils, which appear to be the heavy lifters in the federation on truth and reconciliation. From ceremonies for massacre sites, protection for sacred areas and memorials for significant events, much is committed at the local level. What was important to the communities was that truth-telling is done at their pace, when they are ready and that it is bottom-up. The notion of being compelled to tell your stories without any sense that the telling will be recognised in good faith was of concern. The many recommendations of important commissions and inquiries that have never been implemented are evidence of this.

The most common method of truth-telling espoused by the First Nations dialogues was through the education system. There was a concern that primary school and high school teaching of Aboriginal history was not sufficient or thorough enough. Other approaches, such as memorialising and public art, museums, cultural or educational healing centres and institutions, were also suggested. The primary means would remain through schools and changing school curricula. This truth-telling might be localised and could grow out of an agreement-making process and commence at any time.

8
RESPONSES TO THE ULURU STATEMENT

The Uluru Statement from the Heart immediately attracted national attention once it was issued to the Australian people on 26 May 2017. In the years since, it has been a focal point for debate about how the Constitution should be changed to realise Indigenous aspirations and to build a system of law and government that gives Aboriginal and Torres Strait Islander peoples a say over the issues that affect them.

Despite the strength of the dialogue process underpinning the Statement and strong community support for its recommendations, the Statement has encountered significant obstacles. Some of these emerge from how our politicians have viewed the Statement, others from myths and misconceptions that have grown up around earlier proposals for reform and what the Statement says.

Political responses

On 26 October 2017, four months after the Uluru Convention, Prime Minister Turnbull rejected the idea of the Voice to Parliament. In a statement issued with the Attorney-General and the Minister for Indigenous Affairs, the Prime Minister said, 'The Government does not believe such an addition to our national representative institutions is either desirable or capable of winning acceptance in a referendum'.[1]

He also argued that the Australian democracy is built on 'having equal civic rights' to 'vote for, stand for and serve in' either the House of Representatives or the Senate, and that 'a constitutionally enshrined additional representative assembly for which only Indigenous Australians could vote for or serve in is inconsistent with this fundamental principle'. He said that the Voice 'would inevitably become seen as a third chamber of Parliament'.

Although the Coalition government rejected the Voice to Parliament, there was agreement between the government and the opposition late in 2017 that there would be a Joint Select Committee of Parliament to consider the work of the Referendum Council. This commenced in March 2018. The two co-chairs, Labor Senator Patrick Dodson and Liberal Senator Julian Leeser, presented their interim report on 30 July 2018.

The Labor Party made it party policy to support the Uluru Statement from the Heart and the Voice. They agreed with the Referendum Council that a referendum could be held based on the information from the dialogues, the council report and the decade-long process, and that the details of what the Voice looks like would be deferred to Parliament at a later date. This means Australians could be assured that whatever the model looked like it would have the agreement of the Australian people via Parliament. They committed to put this to a referendum within the first term of a Labor government. The Liberal Party, on the other hand, was persuaded by Patrick Dodson and Julian Leeser that more meat on the bones was required before it could go to a referendum. The Liberal Party election platform stated:

> there needs to be more work done on what model we take to a referendum and what a voice to parliament would be – which is why we are funding a consultation process with Aboriginal and Torres Strait Islander Australians. This process will develop up a question for a referendum and what a referendum will deliver – because no one can answer what a voice to parliament actually is at the moment ...
>
> The key issue that we keep hearing is what is this Voice, the ALP cannot tell us what the Voice might look like and how it might operate. We believe if Australians don't understand what they're voting for in a referendum, they will vote no, and endanger this important issue for another generation.[2]

In its April 2019 budget, the Coalition committed $7.3 million for a co-design process for the Voice to 'improve local and regional decision making' and $160 million for a future referendum once the Voice model has been determined. The funding for the referendum remains in a Contingency Reserve until a referendum model has been determined.

The Coalition was returned to government at the May 2019 election, after Scott Morrison became Prime Minister in 2018. Morrison also dismissed the Voice as a 'third chamber'.

The Dodson and Leeser committee handed down its final report in November 2018. It considered that its 'primary task was to expand on the detail of the proposal for a First Nations Voice'. In this way, it acknowledged the importance of the

Voice. In its final report, the committee recommended that the government 'initiate a process of co-design [of the Voice] with Aboriginal and Torres Strait Islander peoples' that was consistent with its election policy.[3] It also said that the co-design process should:

- consider national, regional and local elements of The Voice and how they interconnect;
- be conducted by a group comprising a majority of Aboriginal and Torres Strait Islander peoples, and officials or appointees of the Australian Government;
- be conducted on a full-time basis and engage with Aboriginal and Torres Strait Islander communities and organisations across Australia, including remote, regional, and urban communities;
- outline and discuss possible options for the local, regional, and national elements of The Voice, including the structure, membership, functions, and operation of The Voice, but with a principal focus on the local bodies and regional bodies and their design and implementation;
- consider the principles, models, and design questions identified by this Committee as a starting point for consultation documents; and
- report to the Government within the term of the 46th Parliament with sufficient time to give The Voice legal form.[4]

Following this process of co-design, the committee recommended that the government 'consider, in a deliberate and timely manner, legislative, executive and constitutional options to establish The Voice'. This approach is known as the two-step or two-phase approach: design the Voice first and then decide the constitutional options for the Voice once there is a model. This is a departure from the approach favoured by the Referendum Council, which argued that a referendum could be held on less detail and that a Voice could be designed after the referendum.

The committee also recommended that the government 'support the process of truth-telling'. It suggested that the government 'consider the establishment, in Canberra, of a National Resting Place, for Aboriginal and Torres Strait Islander remains which could be a place of commemoration, healing and reflection'.

Following the report of the joint select parliamentary committee, the Minister for Indigenous Australians, Ken Wyatt, the first Indigenous person to hold the Indigenous portfolio, announced in October 2019 a 'co-design' process for an 'Indigenous voice to government'. This would be a legislated body rather than a constitutionally entrenched one. Wyatt also announced that he wanted to put a referendum to the Australian public on constitutional recognition within the current term of Parliament.[5] He said that the Morrison Coalition government is 'committed to recognising Indigenous Australians in the constitution and working to achieve this through a process of true co-design'.[6]

It was not made clear what form this referendum would take, and whether this will be a minimalist and symbolic constitutional recognition and how it would work with a legislated Voice – that is, a Voice that is not placed within the Constitution as the Uluru Statement calls for. It could also be that there is a process of legislating the Voice first and then constitutionally enshrining it later.

The 'co-design' process involves a Senior Advisory Group tasked with advising the Minister 'on the co-design process to develop options and models for an Indigenous voice to government'.[7] There is also a National Co-Design Group (which will examine a national Voice, including the structure, operations, functions and membership of such a Voice) and a Local and Regional Co-Design Group (which will develop options for 'local and regional voices'). These groups work alongside public servants and government officials. There is also a 'Senior Officials Group', which consists of representatives from state, territory and federal government and the Australian Local Government Association.

The work of these groups was set out in an interim report released by Wyatt in early 2021. The report described a National Voice as a body of 16 or 18 Indigenous people who would advise Parliament on national issues affecting Aboriginal and Torres Strait Islander peoples. The body could also advise the national government about the development of policy affecting those communities. The National Voice would be limited to providing its views, and could not administer programs or overturn laws or decisions made by the Australian government. The National Voice would be informed by the work of Local and Regional Voices. These bodies would inform the national body of local and regional views, such as how national policies and programs are affecting local communities. This would enable the National Voice to be informed by the experience and views of communities, organisations and even individuals from across Australia.

The interim report also set out a process for consulting with the public about the Voice. It proposed that feedback be sought from all Australians, and in particular Aboriginal and Torres Strait Islander peoples, elders, communities and organisations. The idea was that this would enable the report to be refined for presentation as a set of final recommendations to the Australian government.

There are significant differences between the Wyatt process and that advocated for at the Uluru National Constitutional Convention. There are also differences between Wyatt's approach and Coalition policy.

The Prime Minister, in his Closing the Gap speech on 12 February 2020, said:

> In 2018 the Joint Select Committee on Constitutional Recognition relating to Aboriginal and Torres Strait Islander Peoples delivered a bipartisan report. Our government adopted the four bipartisan recommendations in the report – in particular, recommendation 1: In order to design a voice that best meets the needs and aspirations of Aboriginal and Torres Strait Islander peoples, the Committee recommends a process of co-design between Aboriginal and Torres Strait Islander peoples and government be initiated in communities across Australia to design a voice that can help deliver practical outcomes for that community. This is our government's policy. It is clear from the committee's report that more work needs to be done on a voice proposal.
>
> The government has always supported giving Indigenous people more of a say at the local level. We support the

> process of co-design of the voice because, if we are going to change the lives of Aboriginal and Torres Strait Islander peoples on the ground, we need their buy-in on the matters and policies that affect them. The committee did not make recommendations as to the legal form of the voice – constitutional or legislation. It recommended considering this matter after the process of co-design is completed, and that is what we are doing. We support finalising co-design first.[8]

Despite this, Wyatt is proposing a legislated Voice rather than one enshrined in the Constitution, saying that his 'ambition' is to achieve this before the next election. Wyatt is also proposing a 'Voice to Government', while the Uluru process called for a 'Voice to Parliament'. A Voice to Parliament can compel Parliament, and ultimately the broader community, to listen to the views of Indigenous peoples on matters that affect them. On the other hand, a Voice to Government could be more of an advisory body and is likely to maintain the status quo of the bureaucratic structures that already advise the government.

The Wyatt 'co-design process' is also occurring in a very different way from that envisaged by the Uluru Dialogues and Convention. It was not anticipated that the design of the Voice would be led by a small number of handpicked Indigenous people alongside government agencies and public servants. The Expert Panel involved input from both sides of politics as well as a public submission process for names to the panel. The Referendum Council, similarly, was designed with the input of both sides of politics to maintain bipartisan support. The people involved in the co-design process were chosen by the

Minister alone, with a heavy emphasis on former bureaucrats and those dependent on Commonwealth funding.

The current process places Indigenous peoples (and the rest of the Australian population) as the last groups to be consulted, rather than being active participants in the whole process of design. The individuals involved in the co-design process have been selected by the Minister, and Indigenous peoples more broadly will only be consulted after the proposed model has been endorsed by Cabinet. Given the success of the Regional Dialogues process that led to the Uluru Statement, and the deep and deliberative decision-making shown there, another possibility for design could have been a similar process that centred Indigenous peoples as authors of the Voice design.

Myths and misconceptions

Few Australians know much about the Constitution or the issue of constitutional recognition of Indigenous peoples. Many will not have heard of the Uluru Statement from the Heart. This opens up space for misinformation and misunderstandings, fertile ground for those who oppose change.

The use of exaggeration and misinformation is a regular part of politics, including over constitutional change. For example, one Tasmanian spruiker of Federation in the 1890s was known to end his speeches by saying: 'Gentlemen, if you vote for the Bill you will found a great and glorious nation under the bright Southern Cross, and meat will be cheaper'.[9]

Similarly, opponents of the idea that Australia should become a republic in 1999 argued that a Yes vote would lead to the exclusion of Australia from the Commonwealth (and so be unable to compete in the Commonwealth Games), change the flag, cost taxpayers $900 million, give rise to a Hitler-like presidency, and allow claims by Indigenous people to native title across vast areas of Australia. None of these was true, but they nonetheless formed a large part of the public debate. A similar list of myths and misconceptions is emerging around Indigenous constitutional recognition and the Uluru statement.

Recognition is only symbolism

The word 'recognition' has been conflated with 'symbolism'. Yet recognition in a legal and political context can mean both symbolism *and* substantive changes. The dictionary defines 'recognition' as 'acknowledgment', so some might argue that constitutional recognition should be rejected because it is merely symbolic. The reality is that recognition can mean acknowledgment such as the Expert Panel's statement of recognition, but it can also mean substantive reform to power relations, such as reserved seats or changes to the race power, and it can mean treaty. The fact that constitutional recognition trumps ordinary legislation is why the strongest form of recognition is in a nation's Constitution.

Recognition cedes sovereignty

A broader set of concerns about a recognition referendum comes from Aboriginal and Torres Strait Islander people themselves. Some are concerned that changing the Constitution might frustrate their long-held aspirations for recognition of their sovereignty.

Aboriginal people often say that they did not consent to the taking of their lands and have never given up their rights as a sovereign people. Indeed, many Aboriginal people still assert their sovereignty to this day. The term 'sovereignty' is a widely used but contested term that can mean different things to different people. At its essence, it refers to the claims of Aboriginal people for recognition of their laws and their right to govern their own affairs.

In the *Mabo* case of 1992, the High Court recognised the native title rights of Aboriginal and Torres Strait Islander peoples. However, in later cases, the Court made it clear that this does not amount to recognition of their sovereignty. It said that native title is recognised by Australian law only because it can be accommodated within the common law brought to Australia by the British settlers in 1788. As a result, Australian courts do not recognise that Aboriginal and Torres Strait Islander peoples possess a sovereign law-making power.

Underlying the High Court's reasoning is the view that the sovereignty of Australia's first peoples was displaced by British settlement and the introduction of their law. This was brought about by the assertion by the British of their sovereignty over the Australian continent. All of this occurred before the Australian Constitution came into force in 1901. That document created a new nation upon a continent that the British already regarded as theirs. Changing the Constitution in 1967 did not alter this, nor would changing the Constitution again today.

This represents the position under Australian law, of which the Constitution is the ultimate expression. It does not affect how Aboriginal people view their own sovereignty. As a result, it does not prevent them from asserting their own independence and the continuing validity of their laws and customs.

Quite apart from these arguments, none of the proposed changes to the Constitution, whether it be the Voice to Parliament or a change to the races power, touches upon anything to do with sovereignty. Voting Yes in a recognition referendum would therefore not amount to any surrender of sovereignty, and none of the changes suggests that Aboriginal people are submitting to the nation state or surrendering their claims to self-government. If that was the intention, a different set of words would need to be inserted into the Constitution.

The Uluru Statement from the Heart makes it clear that Aboriginal people never ceded their sovereignty. It says:

> Our Aboriginal and Torres Strait Islander tribes were the first sovereign Nations of the Australian continent and its adjacent islands, and possessed it under our own laws and customs. This our ancestors did, according to the reckoning of our culture, from the Creation, according to the common law from 'time immemorial', and according to science more than 60,000 years ago.
>
> This sovereignty is *a spiritual notion: the ancestral tie between the land, or 'mother nature', and the Aboriginal and Torres Strait Islander peoples who were born therefrom, remain attached thereto, and must one day return thither to be united with our ancestors. This link is the basis of the ownership of the soil, or better, of sovereignty*. It has never been ceded or extinguished, and co-exists with the sovereignty of the Crown.

> How could it be otherwise? That peoples possessed a land for sixty millennia and this sacred link disappears from world history in merely the last two hundred years?
>
> With substantive constitutional change and structural reform, we believe this ancient sovereignty can shine through as a fuller expression of Australia's nationhood.[10]

These words make it clear that sovereignty forms the basis for the Uluru Statement. The reforms set out in a statement are designed to express that sovereignty, rather than to deny it.

A third chamber of Parliament?

In the days after the Uluru Convention, Deputy Prime Minister Barnaby Joyce labelled the Voice a 'new chamber' of Parliament. A few months later, Prime Minister Malcolm Turnbull rejected the Voice by describing it as a 'third chamber' of Parliament and so incompatible with Australia's parliamentary system.

Joyce himself later admitted he may have been mistaken, saying, 'if I got it wrong, I apologise'. Others have also taken issue with the description, including the Joint Select Committee, chaired by Pat Dodson and Julian Leeser, and the Final Report of the Referendum Council.

The Voice is not a chamber of Parliament. It would have no legislative functions. It could not introduce, vote on, or reject legislation. It would, as a result, not in any way fetter the powers of Parliament and is consistent with the notion of parliamentary supremacy. It has none of the features of a chamber of Parliament. As constitutional lawyer Anne Twomey has pointed out, the Voice is not 'a constituent part of the body that makes laws. Its role would be to give a voice to Indigenous views that could be heard within the Parliament'.[11]

An Aboriginal Bill of Rights?

It has been suggested that a recognition referendum arising out of the Expert Panel recommendations would create a Bill of Rights for Aboriginal people. The only aspect of the referendum that might create any form of human rights protection is that connected with prohibiting racial discrimination. If section 116A were included, this would incorporate a new, significant protection into the Constitution. However, this power would only bind the federal Parliament on racial discrimination, nothing more.

A similar answer can be given in regard to the first Joint Select Committee's alternative proposal to insert protection against racial discrimination as a qualifier on a new power to make laws for Aboriginal and Torres Strait Islander peoples. In that form, the protection is more limited again, and would not apply to the whole community, only Aboriginal and Torres Strait Islander peoples. Such protection for them is required, however, because only they could be the subject of special laws enacted under a dedicated federal power. Without clear words stating that this power cannot be used to discriminate, the possibility would remain that the power might be used to impose racial discrimination.

The Voice itself also would not amount to an Aboriginal Bill of Rights. Instead, it would create a new political lever whereby

Indigenous peoples can put their views to the Parliament on issues that affect them.

A right to culture?

It is also said that mentioning Aboriginal culture in the Constitution could lead to several unintended consequences. These include the possibility that judges could be influenced in their sentencing of Aboriginal offenders, and so impose lesser jail sentences, including for serious charges like murder.

Such an argument might perhaps be mounted if the Constitution were to contain a broadly worded and unqualified right to culture. However, no such proposal has been advanced. At most, culture might be mentioned in symbolic words of recognition inserted into the Constitution (something that has been proposed in the past but is not part of the Uluru Statement). This could not lead to the reintroduction of Aboriginal cultural practices. It could also not be used to override criminal laws or to impose new outcomes about the sentencing of Aboriginal offenders. In any event, Australia's criminal laws are mostly state laws, and not federal laws. It is very difficult to see how symbolic recognition of culture in the national Constitution could have any significant effect on these or other similar laws.

Recognition and racial discrimination

One concern that goes to the heart of a recognition referendum is that inserting references to Aboriginal and Torres Strait Islander peoples into the Constitution, such as by words of recognition, a new power or a Voice to Parliament, perpetuates race-based distinctions. This, it is said, runs counter to the idea of removing race-based distinctions from the Constitution.

Mentioning a group of people in the Constitution is not unusual. The document already refers to the people of the Commonwealth and of the particular states on numerous occasions. It does so because the Constitution needs to identify particular peoples for purposes such as voting. State populations are also mentioned specifically in the preamble to the British Act that brought about the Australian Constitution (except for the people of Western Australia, who are not mentioned because they only agreed to join the Federation after the preamble had been drafted).

Making mention of Aboriginal people in the Constitution would be consistent with this. They would be referred to not due to any unscientific sense that they form a distinct racial group, but because it is appropriate that the Constitution mention them as the original inhabitants and first peoples of the Australian continent. The Constitution would recognise them because they have a historical and cultural connection to the land upon which the nation has been founded. Other nations adopt a like approach in rejecting the concept of racial discrimination while making mention of their Indigenous peoples.

For example, section 35 of the Canadian Constitution refers to Indigenous peoples by way of recognising and affirming their 'existing aboriginal and treaty rights'.[12] Similarly, the Indigenous peoples of Scandinavia, the Sami, are recognised in the constitutions of Norway and Finland. The 1814 Constitution of Norway states in article 110A: 'It is the responsibility of the authorities of the State to create conditions enabling the Sami people to preserve and develop its language, culture and way of life'.[13] Section 17 of the 1999 Constitution of Finland provides: 'The Sami, as an indigenous people ... have the right to maintain and develop their own language and culture'.[14] Such constitutions reflect the unique status of Indigenous peoples in the nation.

It is important to consider how this relates to the race power. That power in section 51(xxvi) of the Constitution allows federal legislation to be passed for 'the people of any race for whom it is deemed necessary to make special laws' and has only ever been used to make laws for Aboriginal and Torres Strait Islander peoples. At the Regional Dialogues and Uluru, there was no appetite for removing or amending this provision in the Constitution. Rather, the Voice would 'monitor' the Commonwealth's use of this provision and section 122, the 'territories power'. While something like the Northern Territory intervention might still occur, the existence of the Voice would enable it to be contested and the views of Indigenous people to be heard in the debate. It would thus fill an important function as a counterweight to the race power without establishing race-based distinctions.

9

YES TO THE VOICE?

There is only one way to change the Constitution. The change must be supported by the people voting at a referendum. Australia's referendum record provides good and bad news for those who support the reform.

The good news is that Australians overwhelmingly voted Yes at the last referendum held on Indigenous issues. They did so in 1967 when over 90 per cent of voters granted the federal Parliament power to make laws for Aboriginal people and removed a prohibition on Aboriginal people being counted in the national population. The bad news is that the 1967 poll is exceptional. The larger picture shows a landscape littered with referendum failures. Australians have passed very few proposals at a referendum and none in recent decades.

Changing the Constitution requires high levels of popular support across the nation. This was certainly true of the 1967 referendum and will be true for a constitutional Voice to Parliament.

The response of ordinary Australians to the Voice to Parliament has been very positive. The Reconciliation Barometer is a national survey conducted by Reconciliation Australia every two years to measure and compare attitudes and perceptions towards reconciliation. In the 2020 Barometer, nearly all Australians (95 per cent) want Aboriginal and Torres Strait Islander people to have a say in their own affairs, and more than 80 per cent of the general community believes it is important to protect a First Nations' representative body within the Constitution. Similarly, in 2018, 95 per cent of respondents believed that 'it is important for Aboriginal and Torres Strait Islander people to have a say in matters that affect them' and 80 per cent believed it is important to 'undertake formal truth telling processes'.[1] This demonstrates the consistency of the community response to the Voice to Parliament proposal.

The proposal for a Voice has also received support from organisations as diverse as the Australian Medical Association, the Law Council of Australia and the Australian Council of Social Services. Sporting clubs like Richmond Football Club and codes like the National Rugby League and the Australian Rugby League Commission have endorsed it. As have bodies such as Qantas, Curtin University, Herbert Smith Freehills, King & Wood Mallesons, Fred Hollows Foundation, St Vincent de Paul Society and the Australian College of Rural & Remote Medicine. Many Aboriginal organisations have endorsed the Uluru Statement, such as the Northern Land Council, Central Land Council, the Cape York Land Council and the National Aboriginal Community Controlled Health Organisation.

In 2020, the Centre for Aboriginal Economic Policy Research examined three years of opinion polling on the Voice conducted since June 2017. It found strong support across a majority of states for the Voice, with most polls indicating that 70–75 per cent of Australian voters with a committed position support the reform. Popular support reflected a person's voting intention, with higher levels of support among Green and Labor voters than Coalition and One Nation voters. It concluded that 'a referendum enshrining a First Nations Voice to Parliament could be carried, whichever major party is in government. With bipartisan support, the success of such a referendum is close to guaranteed'.[2]

These polls demonstrate that most Australians support the Voice, but that more work needs to be done to win a referendum. In particular, the chances of success would be greatly strengthened if undecided voters can be convinced of the merits of the reform. This will involve educating more Australians about what the Uluru Statement says, and why it represents a sensible change to the Constitution. It will also be important to ensure that people who support the Voice remain in this camp.

In early 2021, Reconciliation Australia also released its '2021 State of Reconciliation in Australia' report, which provides a snapshot of where reconciliation is placed in Australia.[3] Its conclusion is that reconciliation is growing and that more Australians now understand the impact of colonialism and the modern Australian state on First Nations families and communities. The report concludes that the reconciliation movement in Australia is at a 'tipping point', and that the nation needs to move from 'safe' to 'brave' on issues affecting Aboriginal and Torres Strait Islander peoples. This is further evidence of the growing momentum for substantive change.

This chapter describes how a referendum is held. It also details Australia's prior record of holding referendums. Finally, it explores what needs to be done to give a proposal to recognise Aboriginal and Torres Strait Islander peoples in the Constitution the best chance of success.

How does a referendum work?

Section 128 of the Constitution provides the only way to alter the text of the document. It sets out two steps, which require the coming together of Australia's elected federal representatives and the community at large.

First, a 'proposed law' for changing the text of the Constitution must be passed by the federal Parliament. The normal method is for the proposal to win the support of an absolute majority of both Houses. However, if one House fails to pass it, a special procedure may be invoked whereby the proposal can instead be passed twice by an absolute majority of the members of a single House.

Second, between two and six months after the proposed law has been approved by Parliament, it must be submitted to the people at a referendum. Any person able to vote in federal elections can take part. The proposal must achieve a double majority:

- a majority of people across the nation must vote Yes; and
- a majority of the people in a majority of the states (that is, in at least four out of six states) must vote Yes.

People living in the Australian Capital Territory and the Northern Territory do not get the same vote as other Australians. This is because their vote is only counted in calculating the first majority, and not the second.

The mechanics of holding a referendum are set down in a federal law, the *Referendum (Machinery Provisions) Act 1984*.

Under section 11, the Electoral Commissioner must send each household a pamphlet at least two weeks before voting day showing the proposed amendment to the Constitution, with arguments for and against the proposal of not more than 2000 words each. These for and against arguments are authorised by members of Parliament on each side of the debate. If no parliamentarians vote against the proposal, as occurred in 1967, a No case is not prepared.

The Act also provides for compulsory voting by stating in section 45 that 'it is the duty of every elector to vote at a referendum', with a penalty of up to $50 for failing to do so. Voting takes place in the same way as for a general election. People mark their voting paper in secret in a booth and place their completed vote in a ballot box.

The voting paper sets out the short title of the proposed law, as approved by Parliament, and then asks whether the voter approves the law. They indicate this by writing Yes or No. For example, at the 1999 republic referendum, voters were asked to respond Yes or No to two proposals:

> A proposed law: To alter the Constitution to establish the Commonwealth of Australia as a republic with the Queen and Governor-General being replaced by a President appointed by a two-thirds majority of the members of the Commonwealth Parliament.
>
> A proposed law: To alter the Constitution to insert a preamble.[4]

The referendum record

Since Federation in 1901, 44 referendum proposals have been put to the Australian people. Only eight have succeeded, less than one in five. No referendum has been passed by the people since 1977 when Australians voted, among other things, to set a retirement age of 70 years for High Court judges. As at 2021, 44 years have passed since Australia changed its Constitution. This is by far the longest period that Australia has gone without amending its founding document.

The reasons for the low success rate of referendums are not always easy to identify. It might be thought that referendums are less likely to succeed when held concurrently with a federal election, yet the evidence does not bear this out. Twenty-two of the 44 referendums have been held on election day, with the other half held mid-term. The success rate is identical, with four referendums passed in each case. However, more than 70 years have passed since the last successful election-day referendum in 1946.

It is possible to single out particular states as willing or unwilling to vote Yes. Tasmania has rejected more referendums than any other state (34 out of 44), whereas Western Australia is the only state to have voted Yes in a majority of referendums (23 out of 44). Some of the state voting patterns have changed over time. For example, New South Wales voted against all but three of the 19 proposals put until 1946, but since then has voted for a majority of the proposed changes (14 out of 25), the only state to do so. On the other hand, Western Australia voted Yes to all of the first 13 referendums, while Queensland voted Yes to 15 of the first 17. Yet neither Western Australia nor

Referendums to change the Australian Constitution[5]

Shading indicates a successful referendum

Year	Proposal	Government submitting	States approving	National Yes vote (%)
1906	Senate Elections	Protectionist	6	82.65
1910	Finance	Fusion	3 (Qld, WA, Tas)	49.04
	State Debts	Fusion	5 (all except NSW)	54.95
1911	Legislative Powers	ALP	1 (WA)	39.42
	Monopolies	ALP	1 (WA)	39.89
1913	Trade and Commerce	ALP	3 (Qld, WA, SA)	49.38
	Corporations	ALP	3 (Qld, WA, SA)	49.33
	Industrial Matters	ALP	3 (Qld, WA, SA)	49.33
	Railway Disputes	ALP	3 (Qld, WA, SA)	49.13
	Trusts	ALP	3 (Qld, WA, SA)	49.78
	Nationalisation of Monopolies	ALP	3 (Qld, WA, SA)	49.33
1919	Legislative Powers	Nationalist	3 (Vic, Qld, WA)	49.65
	Nationalisation of Monopolies	Nationalist	3 (Vic, Qld, WA)	48.64
1926	Industry and Commerce	Nat–CP	2 (NSW, Qld)	43.50

Year	Proposal	Government submitting	States approving	National Yes vote (%)
	Essential Services	Nat–CP	2 (NSW, Qld)	42.80
1928	State Debts	Nat–CP	6	74.30
1937	Aviation	UAP	2 (Vic, Qld)	53.56
	Marketing	UAP	0	36.26
1944	Post-war Reconstruction and Democratic Rights	ALP	2 (WA, SA)	45.99
1946	Social Services	ALP	6	54.39
	Organised Marketing	ALP	3 (NSW, Vic, WA)	50.57
	Industrial Employment	ALP	3 (NSW, Vic, WA)	50.30
1948	Rents and Prices	ALP	0	40.66
1951	Communism	Lib–CP	3 (Qld, WA, Tas)	49.44
1967	Parliament	Lib–CP	1 (NSW)	40.25
	Aboriginals	Lib–CP	6	90.77
1973	Prices	ALP	0	43.81
	Incomes	ALP	0	34.42
1974	Simultaneous Elections	ALP	1 (NSW)	48.30

Year	Proposal	Government submitting	States approving	National Yes vote (%)
	Mode of Altering the Constitution	ALP	1 (NSW)	47.99
	Democratic Elections	ALP	1 (NSW)	47.20
	Local Government Bodies	ALP	1 (NSW)	46.85
1977	Simultaneous Elections	Lib–NP	3 (NSW, Vic, SA)	62.22
	Senate Casual Vacancies	Lib–NP	6	73.32
	Referendums	Lib–NP	6	77.72
	Retirement of Judges	Lib–NP	6	80.10
1984	Terms of Senators	ALP	2 (NSW, Vic)	50.64
	Interchange of Powers	ALP	0	47.06
1988	Parliamentary Terms	ALP	0	32.92
	Fair Elections	ALP	0	37.60
	Local Government	ALP	0	33.62
	Rights and Freedoms	ALP	0	30.79
1999	Establishment of Republic	Lib–NP	0	45.13
	Preamble to Constitution	Lib–NP	0	39.34

Queensland (nor South Australia or Tasmania) has supported any referendum since 1977.

The record also reflects the nature of the proposal put to the people. Unsurprisingly, given that referendums can only be initiated by the federal Parliament, most proposals (24 out of 44) have sought to expand Commonwealth power, such as by adding new legislative powers to section 51 of the Constitution over subjects such as industrial relations, employment, monopolies, trusts, essential services, the marketing of primary products, social services, communism, and rents and prices. Australians have overwhelmingly rejected such proposals, with only three succeeding.

The political party in government putting the referendum also plays a major part in explaining the figures. The Australian Labor Party has not succeeded at a referendum since 1946. That referendum, which granted the federal Parliament power over social services such as maternity allowances and unemployment benefits, represents the only time, in 25 attempts, that a Labor government has convinced the Australian people to vote Yes. This success rate of 4 per cent contrasts unfavourably with that of Australia's non-Labor governments. Seven of 19 non-Labor proposals (37 per cent) have been passed, reflecting in part Labor's greater willingness to support referendum proposals from opposition.

It is sometimes suggested that a difficulty arises from the 'majority of States' requirement in section 128; that is, that a majority of voters in a majority of the states must support the proposal. However, only in three instances – two ballots in 1946 and one in 1977 – would this have made any difference. In fact, in every case where a Yes vote prevailed, with the exception of a

1910 referendum, the national majority was accompanied by a Yes vote in every state.

How can we win a referendum?

George Williams and David Hume have undertaken a detailed examination of Australia's referendums in *People Power: The History and Future of the Referendum in Australia*.[6] Their central conclusion is that Australia's referendum record is a result of poor political management, and that the same mistakes have been repeated time and time again. They find that if these errors are avoided, there are good prospects that a referendum will be passed by the Australian people. In particular, reform can be achieved if it is built upon five pillars:

1 multi-party support;
2 popular ownership;
3 popular education;
4 sound and sensible proposals; and
5 a modern referendum process.

1. Multi-party support

Bipartisanship, or multi-party support, has proven to be essential to referendum success. Referendums need support from the major parties at the Commonwealth level.

They also need broad support from the major parties at the state level. The history of referendums in Australia provides many examples of proposals defeated by committed opposition from a major party at either level. This has been a feature of failed referendums put by the Australian Labor Party. Of the 25 proposals it has put to the Australian people, only one has attracted the support of the opposition. That also happens to be the only occasion, in 1946, on which the people passed a proposal put by Labor.

The advocates of constitutional reform have long known of the need for broad political support. The challenge has been how to achieve it. While oppositions can benefit from backing a worthwhile change to the Constitution, it is also very easy for them to oppose an idea. Defeating the government at the ballot not only stymies the government's agenda, but can inflict lasting political damage. In this way, referendums can operate like by-elections. They can be a useful means for an opposition to generate a negative public reaction to the government. Equally, they can enable voters to indicate their dissatisfaction in a way that does not threaten the government's hold on power. State-level parties can also find it easy to oppose a proposal. They can have strong incentives to champion state interests over the national interest.

To secure multi-party support, it is not enough merely to involve a range of political groups in the process; the process must also commit those groups to reform. This can be very difficult to achieve. For example, in 1920 and 1929, the Commonwealth thought it had reached agreement with the states on proposed reforms, but several states backed out and the Commonwealth never put the proposals to the people. Similarly, in 1977, Queensland and Western Australia extricated themselves from an 'agreement' to support simultaneous elections for both Houses of the federal Parliament, which then went on to fail at the ballot box. The problem in each of those cases was a failure to achieve a binding political commitment.

When it comes to Indigenous recognition, the desirability for multi-party support is no less apparent. A referendum on the topic will struggle to succeed without the support of the major parties. Having said that, caution is warranted in comparing past experience as all prior referendums were held when there was no social media and people relied on their newspapers and, eventually, television for political messaging. Even so, an advantage in this respect is that the reform has attracted multi-party support at the federal level, and across all of Australia's states and territories.

A recognition referendum is unusual in that it also requires the backing of another group; the group being 'recognised'. No referendum on this topic can succeed unless it has secured the broad support of the Aboriginal community, and of their leaders. Aboriginal and Torres Strait Islander peoples have been vocal in expressing their strong support for a recognition referendum that includes substantive measures like the Voice.

2. Popular ownership

Just as deadly as partisan opposition is the perception that a constitutional reform idea is a 'politicians' proposal'. From proposals which have been felled by the cry of 'no more politicians', to the republic referendum in 1999, which was killed off by the claim that it was the 'politicians' republic', Australians have consistently voted No when they believe a proposal is motivated by politicians' self-interest. This reflects a well-known undercurrent of distrust by Australians of their elected representatives.

The design of the referendum process exacerbates this problem. Politicians, and only politicians, can initiate constitutional reform through the federal Parliament. This renders every proposal at risk of being perceived as self-serving, especially of those interests aligned with the Commonwealth.

Popular ownership is difficult to achieve. It cuts against the grain of how Australian politics normally works, where politicians are only too ready to claim ownership of reforms and successes. Popular ownership was achieved in the 1967 referendum because it emerged out of a long-running peoples' movement.

On that occasion, the referendum was held not because the prime minister of the day saw it as a priority, but as a response to a popular demand for change that had been building for decades. The Voice is also generating strong community backing and involvement. This takes time and higher levels of community engagement. It has only been since 2017 that the Voice emerged as the preferred – indeed, as many people see it, the only – option for effective constitutional recognition that is both symbolic and substantive. By contrast, the 1967 referendum had a clearer path because from an early stage it was focused on the two clauses in the Constitution that excluded Aboriginal people.

The task now for those who support the Voice is to continue to build a strong community base for change. Without this, there is a danger that the referendum will be a politician-led process. This will jeopardise the chances of success. The referendum is not likely to pass if people view it as being a politicians' proposal.

At the Regional Dialogues and at the Uluru National

Convention, the consensus decision reached – for Voice, Treaty, Truth – was important precisely because there was a sense of popular ownership of the decision among Indigenous peoples. This now needs to be realised in the broader Australian community to give a referendum the best chance of success.

There is no one way of engendering broad popular ownership. But popular participation is essential, both in the process of generating ideas, and the consultation and deliberation that follows. This might include:

- extended national and grassroots debate and consultation about the wording of the proposal, such as through the work of parliamentary committees, community groups, local government and campaigning organisations;
- debate and consultation across a wide variety of forums, such as through an elected constitutional convention, a series of Indigenous conventions or a randomly selected group of Australians coming together as a citizens' assembly; and
- a process that makes full use of available media, including television, radio, newspapers and new technologies not available in previous referendums such as social media.

Some of these things are occurring now, but clearly more is needed to ensure that political leadership in favour of the reform is matched by broad and deep community engagement.

The republic referendum was preceded by a constitutional convention. Conventions have proved to be the most successful ways of debating constitutional reform and building momentum towards a Yes vote at a referendum. In the case of the republic convention in 1998, it generated a huge amount of attention and it built general awareness for the referendum campaign. However, the process for selecting delegates was flawed, with only half the delegates chosen by the people, and the other half being appointees (mostly chosen by the government). This meant the outcome – of modest change – was disputed by some republicans, who then advocated a No vote. This was a major factor in the 1999 referendum returning a No vote. The example provides a strong lesson in both the benefits of a convention, and in how a poorly designed convention can undermine the chances of success.

3. Popular education

Surveys of the Australian public show a disturbing lack of knowledge about the Constitution and Australian government. Many Australians know little of even the most basic aspects of government. This is often a reflection of citizens being disengaged from many aspects of their democracy. The problem has been demonstrated over many years.

A 1987 survey for the Constitutional Commission found that almost half the population did not realise Australia has a Constitution, with the figure being nearly 70 per cent of Australians aged between 18 and 24. In 2015, a survey showed that only 65 per cent of the population knew that Australia had a Constitution. Other reports have shown that only one in five people had some understanding of what the Constitution contained, while more than a quarter named the Supreme Court, not the High Court, as the 'top' court in Australia. Finally, in 2006, Amnesty International Australia commissioned a nationwide poll of 1001 voters by Roy Morgan Research, in which, remarkably, 61 per cent said they thought Australia has a national Bill of Rights.

The results suggest that many Australians know more about the United States system of government than our own, perhaps in part because of the prevalence of US popular culture. This can produce confusion about how the Australian system works, as many people assume that the Australian system is the same as that of the United States.

These problems can be telling during a referendum campaign. A lack of knowledge, or false knowledge, on the part of the voter, can translate into a misunderstanding of a proposal, a potential to be manipulated by the Yes or No cases, and even an unwillingness to consider change on the basis that 'don't know, vote No' is the best policy. Misunderstanding the Constitution can mean that people can cast a Yes or No vote to a proposal in a way that does not reflect their real intentions. Hence, a person may vote No out of concern about what the proposal might do, even where they would have supported the proposal had they fully understood it.

Overall, the record shows that when voters do not understand or have no opinion on a proposal, they tend to vote No. Polls from the 1999 referendum showed that many people had not read the official pamphlet distributed by the Commonwealth to explain the proposals, and that people who had not read the pamphlet were far more likely to vote No. Polling in the lead-up to the 1967, 1977 and 1988 referendums also suggested that those who did not know which way they would vote shortly before the referendum swung heavily into the No column on the day of the vote.

Information also needs to reach a variety of different groups in Australia to ensure all Australians are educated about the reforms. As an example, in November 2020, SBS released translations of the Uluru Statement from the Heart in 65 languages.

Governments will never be entirely effective at educating Australians about the Constitution and the referendum process. The Constitution is a complex legal document. Nevertheless, Australians need access to information about their system of government and any proposal for reform. The community will require sufficient information about Indigenous recognition so that they are not vulnerable to false arguments and scare campaigns. This means that people must have access not only to the arguments of the advocates, but also to credible, independent information that explains how the Constitution and their system of government works. This knowledge is essential so that people can properly assess the Yes and No cases. If Australians are to vote Yes, they will need to feel safe and confident in doing so.

4. Sound and sensible proposals

As important as it is to get the process of generating proposals right, it is equally important to get the proposals themselves right. A change to the Constitution is for the long term. It is extremely hard to undo, and could be in place for the next 50 to 100 years. As a result, people are understandably prepared to vote No if they detect even the slightest flaw with the proposal. For example, at the 1999 referendum on a republic, some people decided to vote No because of concerns that there was a flaw in the way that an Australian President might have been dismissed.

The proposal must also be necessary. Australians typically want to know that they are voting on a change that is needed to fix some sort of problem. It should be necessary in a practical sense. Otherwise, voters are wont to ask, why are so many millions of dollars of taxpayers' money being spent on the idea? Where this hurdle has not been overcome, people have often been influenced by the mantra 'if it ain't broke, don't fix it'.

Good proposals can be generated where they are based upon past experimentation and practice. Australians are more likely to agree to such changes. Successful proposals in 1928, 1946, 1967 and 1977 were all based, to a greater or lesser extent, upon people being asked to ratify pre-existing arrangements.

The Australian states can play a role. Successful state reform makes the effects of national constitutional change much less of an unknown. It makes change incremental, rather than abrupt. It can also turn those states that have adopted the reform (and people in those states) into advocates of the reform.

Many of the proposals for constitutional change reflect existing laws and past experimentation in Australia. Symbolic recognition has already been inserted into a majority of the state constitutions. Protection from racial discrimination has also existed since 1975 in the *Racial Discrimination Act*. Courts have applied that law for four decades to prevent state and territory laws from discriminating on the basis of race, especially against Aboriginal and Torres Strait Islander people. The Voice also has a range of antecedents. There are many examples of bodies that have been established to advise parliaments about specific matters, such as advice on human rights issues by the Australian

Human Rights Commission. The Voice would be a special and important new point of advice to Parliament, but hardly a novel and untested initiative.

5. A modern referendum process

The system for the holding of referendums is set out in the *Referendum (Machinery Provisions) Act*. That law was adopted in 1912, and has changed little since. It was designed at a time when Australia's population was far smaller and far less diverse, and the print media and public speeches were the main modes of communication.

As a result, the law only enables voters to receive Yes and No case information in print form. There is no provision for other means of communication, such as via social media or the internet generally. Indeed, any referendum on constitutional recognition or the Voice will be the first referendum held in the social media age, and this may pose new and significant questions for how to engage voters and promote the Yes and No cases.

The Act also forces the Commonwealth to hold a referendum with one arm tied behind its back. It does this by preventing the Commonwealth from spending any money on advocating the change. On the other hand, there is no such restriction on any other person or organisation, including a state or territory government, from spending its money to oppose the change.

The law is showing its age and needs to be updated. A number of changes to modernise the way that Australia holds referendums have been suggested. These include:

- abolishing the expenditure restrictions on the federal government;
- providing funds, fairly distributed, to campaigns representing those who support and oppose the referendum;
- allowing the official Yes/No pamphlet to be distributed electronically; and
- providing voters with neutral information to help them understand the Constitution and the proposed reform.

It will be much harder to win a recognition referendum unless changes such as these are made. It is important, though, that this occurs well before a referendum is held. The changes raise important issues of public policy that could affect any future referendum, and must not be rushed through Parliament on the eve of a referendum vote. If nothing else, leaving such changes to the last minute may pose a political problem. They are likely to give rise to disagreement between the political parties, which may undermine both the perception and reality of multi-party support for the impending referendum.

The coming vote

Australia's long record of failed attempts at constitutional reform does not mean that winning a referendum today is 'mission impossible'. Instead, it only shows that we should expect a referendum to fail whenever the nation's major political parties disagree, or when poor management by our leaders means that the Australian people feel left out or confused about what is being changed. People will also vote No to a proposal that is dangerous or has been poorly thought out. A lot of this, of course, is common sense, yet the referendum record displays a tendency to repeat these same mistakes time and time again.

Changing Australia's Constitution to recognise Aboriginal and Torres Strait Islander peoples and create a Voice to Parliament is achievable. If nothing else, we should not forget the 1967 referendum. Not only was that referendum passed, the Yes vote reached a record high in securing over 90 per cent support from the Australian people. That momentous national vote shows what is possible if the right proposal to change the Constitution is put to the Australian people in the right way.

In many ways, this referendum is about Australia continuing its journey of coming to terms with its past. The Cherbourg community in Queensland is an example of this. They have reclaimed their old Ration Shed, a dwelling symbolising an era in which Aboriginal people were discriminated against and denied basic freedoms, transforming it into the centrepiece of a thriving cultural precinct.

In the same way, a recognition referendum offers the opportunity to recast the Australian Constitution. If a sound proposal is put forward, and the people vote Yes, the Constitution can be renovated from a document that is silent about the Aboriginal and Torres Strait Islander history of this continent and which permits discrimination on the basis of race. As the Uluru Statement from the Heart says, in 1967, Aboriginal and Torres Strait Islander people 'were counted, in 2017 we seek to be heard'.

Appendix
ULURU STATEMENT FROM THE HEART

We, gathered at the 2017 National Constitutional Convention, coming from all points of the southern sky, make this statement from the heart:

Our Aboriginal and Torres Strait Islander tribes were the first sovereign Nations of the Australian continent and its adjacent islands, and possessed it under our own laws and customs. This our ancestors did, according to the reckoning of our culture, from the Creation, according to the common law from 'time immemorial', and according to science more than 60 000 years ago.

This sovereignty is *a spiritual notion: the ancestral tie between the land, or 'mother nature', and the Aboriginal and Torres Strait Islander peoples who were born therefrom, remain attached thereto, and must one day return thither to be united with our ancestors. This link is the basis of the ownership of the soil, or better, of sovereignty*. It has never been ceded or extinguished, and co-exists with the sovereignty of the Crown.

How could it be otherwise? That peoples possessed a land for sixty millennia and this sacred link disappears from world history in merely the last two hundred years?

With substantive constitutional change and structural reform, we believe this ancient sovereignty can shine through as a fuller expression of Australia's nationhood.

Proportionally, we are the most incarcerated people on the planet. We are not an innately criminal people. Our children are aliened from their families at unprecedented rates. This cannot be because we have no love for them. And our youth languish in detention in obscene numbers. They should be our hope for the future.

These dimensions of our crisis tell plainly the structural nature of our problem. This is *the torment of our powerlessness*.

We seek constitutional reforms to empower our people and take *a rightful place* in our own country. When we have power over our destiny our children will flourish. They will walk in two worlds and their culture will be a gift to their country.

We call for the establishment of a First Nations Voice enshrined in the Constitution.

Makarrata is the culmination of our agenda: *the coming together after a struggle*. It captures our aspirations for a fair and truthful relationship with the people of Australia and a better future for our children based on justice and self-determination.

We seek a Makarrata Commission to supervise a process of agreement-making between governments and First Nations and truth-telling about our history.

In 1967 we were counted, in 2017 we seek to be heard. We leave base camp and start our trek across this vast country. We invite you to walk with us in a movement of the Australian people for a better future.

ACKNOWLEDGMENTS

The authors thank Sophie Rigney for her assistance in the preparation of this book.

The authors also acknowledge those who assisted with their earlier work *Everything You Need to Know about the Referendum to Recognise Indigenous Australians*. Parts of this book are based upon that earlier publication.

NOTES

Introduction

1 Beryl Gambrill, Submission No. 127 to the Expert Panel on Constitutional Recognition of Indigenous Australians, 10 August 2011.
2 Royal Australian and New Zealand College of Psychiatrists, 'Mental Health Benefits in Constitutional Recognition of Indigenous Australians', Media Release, 25 May 2011. See also Royal Australian and New Zealand College of Psychiatrists, 'Recognition of Indigenous People in the Australian Constitution', Position Statement No. 68, September 2011.

1 – Making the Constitution

1 Bill Gammage, *The Biggest Estate on Earth: How Aborigines Made Australia*, Allen & Unwin, Sydney, 2011, p. 2.
2 Secret Instructions from Lord Morton to Lieutenant James Cook, 30 July 1768.
3 Raymond Evans, *A History of Queensland*, Cambridge University Press, Melbourne, 2007, p. 18.
4 Draught Instructions from Lord Sydney to Governor Phillip, 25 April 1787.
5 Expert Panel on Constitutional Recognition of Indigenous Australians, *Recognising Aboriginal and Torres Strait Islander Peoples in the Constitution: Report of the Expert Panel*, Report, 16 January 2012, pp. 1–3.
6 Russel Ward, *Concise History of Australia*, University of Queensland Press, Brisbane (first published 1965), 1992, p. 56.
7 Garth Nettheim et al., *Indigenous Legal Issues*, 4th edition, Thomson Reuters, Sydney, 2009, p. 21.
8 David Neal, *The Rule of Law in a Penal Colony: Law and Power in Early New South Wales*, Cambridge University Press, Melbourne, 1991, p. 17.
9 Sir Henry Parkes, 'Tenterfield Oration', Speech delivered at the Tenterfield School of Arts, 24 October 1889.
10 Margaret Jolly, *Family and Gender in the Pacific: Domestic Contradictions and the Colonial Impact*, Cambridge University Press, Melbourne, 1989, p. 239.
11 *Official Record of the Debates of the Australasian Federal Convention: 1891–1898* (Convention Debates), Melbourne, 3 March 1898, p. 1784 (John Quick). Dr Quick also refers to 'people of any undesirable race or of undesirable antecedents': Convention Debates, Melbourne, 2 March 1898, p. 1752.

12 *Commonwealth of Australia Constitution Act 1900* (Imp) 63 & 64 Vict, preamble.
13 Australian Constitution section 127, as repealed by *Constitution Alteration (Aboriginals) 1967* (Cth) section 3.
14 *Official Record of the Debates of the Australasian Federal Convention: 1891–1898*, 8 February 1898, Melbourne, p. 713 (Edmund Barton).
15 Australian Constitution section 51(xxvi), later amended by *Constitution Alteration (Aboriginals) 1967* (Cth) section 2.
16 Harrison Moore, *The Constitution of the Commonwealth of Australia*, 2nd edition, Maxwell, Melbourne, 1910, p. 464.
17 *Official Record of the Debates of the National Australasian Convention*, Sydney (2 March – 9 April 1891), 8 April 1891, p. 703 (Sir Samuel Griffith).
18 *Official Record of the Debates of the Australasian Federal Convention: 1891–1898*, Melbourne, 27 January 1898, pp. 228–29 (Edmund Barton).
19 John Quick and Robert Garran, *The Annotated Constitution of the Australian Commonwealth*, Angus & Robertson, Sydney, 1901, p. 622.
20 *Official Record of the Debates of the Australasian Federal Convention: 1891–1898*, Melbourne, 28 January 1898, p. 250 (Josiah Symon).
21 John Quick and Robert Garran, *The Annotated Constitution of the Australian Commonwealth*, Angus & Robertson, Sydney, 1901, p. 623.
22 *Official Record of the Debates of the Australasian Federal Convention: 1891–1898*, Melbourne, 27 January 1898, p. 240 (Sir John Forrest).
23 *Official Record of the Debates of the Australasian Federal Convention: 1891–1898*, Melbourne, 8 February 1898, pp. 665–66 (Sir John Forrest).
24 *Official Record of the Debates of the Australasian Federal Convention: 1891–1898*, Melbourne, 3 March 1898, p. 1801 (Henry Higgins).
25 *Immigration Restriction Act 1901* (Cth) section 3(a).
26 Commonwealth, Parliamentary Debates, House of Representatives, 26 September 1901, p. 5233 (Edmund Barton).
27 Nick O'Neill et al., *Retreat from Injustice: Human Rights Law in Australia*, Federation Press, Sydney, 2004, p. 698, citing John Lack and Jacqueline Templeton (eds), *Sources of Australian Immigration History 1901–1945*, University of Melbourne, Melbourne, 1988, pp. 11–12.
28 Commonwealth, Parliamentary Debates, House of Representatives, 24 April 1902, p. 11979 (Isaac Isaacs).
29 *Ibid.*, p. 11977 (Henry Higgins).
30 *Commonwealth Franchise Act 1902* (Cth) section 4.
31 Gordon Reid, *That Unhappy Race: Queensland and the Aboriginal Problem, 1838–1901*, Australian Scholarly Publishing, Melbourne, 2006, p. ix.

2 – The 1967 referendum

1 Bain Attwood and Andrew Markus, *The 1967 Referendum: Race, Power and the Australian Constitution*, 2nd edition, Aboriginal Studies Press, Canberra, 2007, p. 7.

2 John Gardiner-Garden, *The 1967 Referendum – History and Myths*, Research Brief No. 11, Parliamentary Library, 2006–07, p. 5.

3 AIATSIS, 'We Hereby Make Protest', <aiatsis.gov.au/explore/day-of-mourning>.

4 The Universal Declaration of Human Rights 1948, preamble.

5 John Gardiner-Garden, *The 1967 Referendum – History and Myths*, Research Brief No. 11, Parliamentary Library, 2006–07, p. 72.

6 Commonwealth, Parliamentary Debates, House of Representatives, 9 May 1957, p. 1227 (HV Evatt).

7 Bain Attwood and Andrew Markus, *The 1967 Referendum: Race, Power and the Australian Constitution*, 2nd edition, Aboriginal Studies Press, Canberra, 2007, p. 23.

8 Expert Panel on Constitutional Recognition of Indigenous Australians, *Recognising Aboriginal and Torres Strait Islander Peoples in the Constitution: Report of the Expert Panel*, Report, 16 January 2012, p. 21.

9 Geoffrey Sawer, 'The Australian Constitution and the Australian Aborigine', 1966, *Federal Law Review*, vol. 2, p. 26; Australian Bureau of Statistics, *Aboriginal and Torres Strait Islander Peoples and The Census after the 1967 Referendum*, <https://www.abs.gov.au/ausstats/abs@.nsf/Previousproducts/2071.0Feature%20Article2July%202011?opendocument&tabname=Summary&prodno=2071.0&issue=July%202011&num=&view=>.

10 *The Age*, 22 May 1967, p. 5.

11 *Ibid.*

12 Bain Attwood and Andrew Markus, *The 1967 Referendum: Race, Power and the Australian Constitution*, 2nd edition, Aboriginal Studies Press, Canberra, 2007, pp. 30, 130.

13 *Ibid.*, p. 47.

14 Robert French, 'The Race Power: A Constitutional Chimera', in HP Lee and George Winterton (eds), *Australian Constitutional Landmarks*, Cambridge University Press, Melbourne, 2003, p. 190.

15 Geoffrey Sawer, 'The Australian Constitution and the Australian Aborigine', 1967, *Federal Law Review*, vol. 2, p. 35.

16 Bain Attwood and Andrew Markus, *The 1967 Referendum: Race, Power and the Australian Constitution*, 2nd edition, Aboriginal Studies Press, Canberra, 2007, p. 114.

17 George Williams and David Hume, *People Power: The History and Future of the Referendum in Australia*, UNSW Press, Sydney, 2010, p. 149.

18 *Parliamentary Handbook of the Commonwealth of Australia 2011*, 32nd edition, Parliamentary Library, Department of Parliamentary Services, 2011, p. 388.

19 *The Australian*, 29 May 1967, p. 1.

20 *Ibid.*

21 *Sunday Herald*, 28 May 1967, p. 1.

22 Bain Attwood and Andrew Markus, *The 1967 Referendum: Race, Power and the Australian Constitution*, 2nd edition, Aboriginal Studies Press, Canberra, 2007, p. 57.
23 Jackie Huggins, 'The 1967 Referendum … Four Decades Later', Speech delivered for The Sydney Institute, 22 May 2007.
24 Bain Attwood and Andrew Markus, *The 1967 Referendum: Race, Power and the Australian Constitution*, 2nd edition, Aboriginal Studies Press, Canberra, 2007, p. 57.
25 *Ibid.*, p. 62.

3 – A new era?

1 Jack Horner, *Seeking Racial Justice: An Insider's Memoir of the Movement for Aboriginal Advancement*, Aboriginal Studies Press, Canberra, 2004, pp. 133–34.
2 *Ibid.*, p. 143.
3 Larissa Behrendt, 'Preface' in Gary Foley, Andrew Schaap and Edwina Howell (eds), *The Aboriginal Tent Embassy: Sovereignty, Black Power, Land Rights and the State*, Routledge, London, 2013, p. xxiii.
4 National Museum of Australia, *Campaigning for Land Rights, 1963–68* (Collaborating for Indigenous Rights), <www.nma.gov.au/explore/features/indigenous-rights/land-rights/campaigning>.
5 Jack Horner, *Seeking Racial Justice: An Insider's Memoir of the Movement for Aboriginal Advancement*, Aboriginal Studies Press, Canberra, 2004, p. 138.
6 The People of Yirrkala, 'Yolngu Statement in the Gupapunyngu Language', 6 May 1971, <www.kooriweb.org/foley/resources/pdfs/126.pdf>.
7 *Milirrpum v Nabalco Pty Ltd* (1971) 17 Federal Law Reports 141 at 267.
8 The People of Yirrkala, 'Yolngu Statement in the Gupapunyngu Language'.
9 Gary Foley, Andrew Schaap and Edwina Howell (eds), *The Aboriginal Tent Embassy: Sovereignty, Black Power, Land Rights and the State*, Routledge, London, 2013, p. xxv.
10 *Ibid.*, p. xxiii.
11 Gough Whitlam, Speech delivered at the Gurindji Land Ceremony, 16 August 1975, <pmtranscripts.pmc.gov.au/release/transcript-3849>.
12 *Coe v Commonwealth* (1979) 24 Australian Law Reports, p. 122.
13 LR Hiatt, 'Treaty, Compact, Makarrata …?', *Oceania*, 1987, no. 58, p. 140.
14 Senate Standing Committee on Constitutional and Legal Affairs on the Feasibility of a Compact or 'Makarrata' between the Commonwealth and Aboriginal People, Senate of Australia, *Two Hundred Years Later …*, 1983, p. 115.
15 Australian Constitutional Commission, *Final Report of the Constitutional Commission*, 1988, vol. 1, para. 4.158.
16 *Ibid.*, para. 10.372.
17 *Ibid.*, para. 10.455.
18 Editorial, 'World Focus on Aborigines', *Sydney Morning Herald*, 19 January 1988.

19 Peter Cochrane and David Goodman, 'The Great Australian Journey: Cultural Logic and Nationalism in the Postmodern Era', *Australian Historical Studies*, 1988, vol. 23, no. 91, p. 25.
20 'Barunga Statement', *Aboriginal Law Bulletin*, 1988, vol. 2, no. 33, p. 16.
21 *Ibid.*
22 Prime Minister Robert Hawke, Speech delivered at the Barunga Sports and Cultural Festival, Northern Territory, 12 June 1988, <pmtranscripts.pmc.gov.au/sites/default/files/original/00007334.pdf>.
23 Murray Goot and Tim Rowse, *Divided Nation?: Indigenous Affairs and the Imagined Public*, Melbourne University Publishing, Melbourne, 2007, p. 77.
24 Murray Goot and Tim Rowse, *Divided Nation?: Indigenous Affairs and the Imagined Public*, Melbourne University Publishing, Melbourne, 2007, p. 77, citing ABC TV, *Four Corners*, 17 March 1986 (Patrick Dodson).
25 'Treaty', Yothu Yindi, Sony/ATV Music Publishing, 1991.
26 *Council for Aboriginal Reconciliation Act 1991* (Cth), preamble.
27 Damien Short, *Reconciliation and Colonial Power: Indigenous Rights in Australia*, Ashgate, Aldershot, 2008, p. 132.
28 Gary Foley, Andrew Schaap and Edwina Howell (eds), *The Aboriginal Tent Embassy: Sovereignty, Black Power, Land Rights and the State*, Routledge, London, 2013, p. 193, citing Margaret Meenaghan, Interview with Kevin Gilbert, 1992.
29 *Council for Aboriginal Reconciliation Act 1991* (Cth), preamble.
30 Prime Minister Paul Keating, 'Opportunity and Care, Dignity and Hope', Speech delivered at Australia's celebration of the 1993 International Year of the World's Indigenous Peoples, Redfern Park, 10 December 1992, <antar.org.au/sites/default/files/paul_keating_speech_transcript.pdf>.
31 *Mabo v Queensland* (No. 2) (1992) 175 Commonwealth Law Reports, p. 1.
32 Robert Manne, 'The Howard Years: A Political Interpretation', in Robert Manne (ed.), *The Howard Years*, Black Inc Agenda, Melbourne, 2004, p. 18.
33 Prime Minister John Howard, Speech delivered at the opening ceremony of the Australian Reconciliation Convention, Melbourne, 26 May 1997.
34 Jeremy Cordeaux, Interview with Prime Minister John Howard, 5DN, 5 March 1999, <pmtranscripts.pmc.gov.au/release/transcript-11182>.
35 Commonwealth, Parliamentary Debates, House of Representatives, 26 August 1999, p. 9205 (Prime Minister John Howard).
36 *Kartinyeri v Commonwealth (Hindmarsh Island Bridge Case)*, Transcript of Argument, High Court of Australia, 5 February 1998.
37 Australian Constitutional Convention, *Report of the Constitutional Convention*, Department of Prime Minister and Cabinet, 1998, vol. 3, p. 10.
38 'Recent Documents: Final Resolutions of the Constitutional Convention, Canberra, 2–13 February 1998', 1998, *Public Law Review*, vol. 9, p. 57.
39 Council of Aboriginal Reconciliation, *Going Forward: Social Justice for the First Australians*, AGPS, Canberra, 1995, p. 36.
40 Parliament of Australia, Constitutional Alteration (Preamble) 1999, No. 32 of 1999, 11 August 1999.

41 Helen Lambert, 'A Draft Preamble: Les Murray and the Politics of Poetry', *Journal of Australian Studies*, 2003, no. 27, vol. 80, p. 8, citing Paul Sheehan, 'A Redneck Enjoys the Glow of his Afterlife', *Sydney Morning Herald*, 2 October 1999.
42 Prime Minister John Howard and Senator Aden Ridgeway, Joint Press Conference, 3 November 1999.
43 Constitutional Alteration (Preamble) Bill 1999 (Cth).
44 ABC Television, 'New Constitution Preamble', *7.30 Report*, 11 August 1999 (Gatjil Djerrkura).
45 ABC Television, 'New Constitution Preamble', *7.30 Report*, 11 August 1999 (Senator Aden Ridgeway).
46 ABC Local Radio, 'Aboriginal Leaders Call for "No" Vote on Preamble', *The World Today*, 3 November 1999 (Peter Yu), <www.abc.net.au/worldtoday/stories/s64063.htm>.
47 Margo Kingston, 'Howard Keen to Reconcile', *Sydney Morning Herald*, 9 November 1999, cited in Mark McKenna, Amelia Simpson and George Williams, 'With Hope in God, the Prime Minister and the Poet: Lessons from the 1999 Referendum on the Preamble', *University of New South Wales Law Journal*, 2001, vol. 24, p. 416.
48 Gatjil Djerrkura, 'Lack of Proper Consultation Sinks Referendum', ATSIC Media Release, 8 November 1999.
49 Constitution Alteration (Preamble) 1999 (Cth) cl 125A.
50 Mark McKenna, Amelia Simpson and George Williams, 'First Words: The Preamble to the Australian Constitution', *University of New South Wales Law Journal*, 2001, vol. 24, p. 386.
51 Council for Aboriginal Reconciliation, *Reconciliation: Australia's Challenge*, Final Report to the Prime Minister and the Commonwealth Parliament, December 2000, ch. 10.
52 *Ibid.*
53 Sir William Deane, 'Address to Corroboree 2000', Speech delivered on the occasion of Corroboree 2000, Sydney, 27 May 2000, <australianpolitics.com/2000/05/27/governor-general-sir-william-deane-address-to-corroboree-2000.html>.
54 Council for Aboriginal Reconciliation, *The People's Movement*, AustLII, <www5.austlii.edu.au/au/orgs/car/council/spl98_20/goal3.htm>.
55 'Some Marched Alone in Crowd', *Canberra Times*, 3 June 2000, p. 3.
56 John Laws, Interview with John Howard, Prime Minister of Australia, Sydney, 29 May 2000.
57 Debra Jopson, 'Surge in Support for Treaty with Aborigines', *Sydney Morning Herald*, 8 November 2000.
58 Council for Aboriginal Reconciliation, *Reconciliation: Australia's Challenge*, Final Report to the Prime Minister and the Commonwealth Parliament, December 2000, ch. 10.

4 – The journey to recognition

1 *Constitution Act 1975* (Vic) section 1A.
2 *Constitution Act 1934* (SA) section 2(3).
3 John Howard, 'A New Reconciliation', *The Sydney Papers*, 2007, vol. 19, no. 4, 104 at pp. 108–109.
4 Commonwealth, Parliamentary Debates, House of Representatives, 13 February 2008, p. 167 (Kevin Rudd).
5 *Ibid.*, p. 172.
6 Commonwealth, *Australia 2020 Summit: Final Report*, Department of the Prime Minister and Cabinet, 2008, p. 231.
7 *Communiqué from Yolngu and Bininj Leaders at Yirrkala to the Australian Government*, Yolngu and Bininj Leaders' Statement of Intent, 23 July 2008.
8 *Ibid.*
9 Prime Minister Kevin Rudd, 'Joint Press Conference with the Chief Minister of the Northern Territory, Paul Henderson', Press Release, 24 July 2008.
10 Natasha Robinson and Samantha Maiden, 'No Rush to Indigenous Amendment to Constitution', *The Australian*, 25 July 2008.
11 Expert Panel on Constitutional Recognition of Indigenous Australians, *Recognising Aboriginal and Torres Strait Islander Peoples in the Constitution: Report of the Expert Panel*, Report, 16 January 2012, 'Executive Summary', p. xi.
12 *Ibid.*, p. xviii.
13 *Aboriginal and Torres Strait Islander Peoples Recognition Act 2013* (Cth) section 3.
14 Commonwealth, Parliamentary Debates, House of Representatives, 13 February 2013, p. 1123.
15 *Ibid.*
16 Patricia Karvelas, 'Historic Constitution Vote over Indigenous Recognition Facing Hurdles', *The Australian* (online), 20 January 2012, <www.theaustralian.com.au/national-affairs/indigenous/historic-constitution-vote-over-indigenous-recognition-facing-hurdles/news-story/92c14ff592d43981049fdade4280ddbf>.
17 Prime Minister Tony Abbott, 'Australia Day 2014', Media Release and Speech, 26 January 2014.
18 Bill Shorten, 'Keynote Address at the Garma Festival', Arnhem, Northern Territory, 3 August 2014.
19 Nigel Scullion, 'Next Step Towards Indigenous Constitutional Recognition', 28 March 2014, <www.indigenous.gov.au/minister-scullion-next-step-towards-indigenous-constitutional-recognition>.
20 Australian National Audit Office, 'Performance Audit Report: Indigenous Advancement Strategy' 3 February 2017, <www.anao.gov.au/work/performance-audit/indigenous-advancement-strategy>.
21 'Statement Presented by Aboriginal and Torres Strait Islander Attendees at a Meeting Held with the Prime Minister and Opposition Leader on

Constitutional Recognition', 6 July 2015, HC Coombs Centre, Kirribilli, Sydney, <www.austlii.edu.au/au/journals/ILB/2015/37.pdf>.

5 – What did the Expert Panel recommend?

1 Constitution Alteration (Preamble) Bill 1999 (Cth).
2 Joint Select Committee on Constitutional Recognition of Aboriginal and Torres Strait Islander Peoples, Parliament of Australia, *Interim Report*, 2014, p. 29.
3 *Commonwealth of Australia Constitution Act 1900* (Imp) 63 & 64 Vict, preamble.
4 Expert Panel on Constitutional Recognition of Indigenous Australians, *Recognising Aboriginal and Torres Strait Islander Peoples in the Constitution: Report of the Expert Panel*, Report, 16 January 2012, 'Executive Summary', p. xviii.
5 Indigenous Youth Engagement Council, 'RECOGNISE THIS', Youth Report on Constitutional Recognition, National Centre of Indigenous Excellence Indigenous Youth Engagement Council, 2013, p. 31.
6 Joint Select Committee on Constitutional Recognition of Aboriginal and Torres Strait Islander Peoples, Parliament of Australia, *Interim Report*, 2014, p. 26.
7 Constitution, sections 25, 51(xxvi).
8 *Ibid.*, section 24.
9 Expert Panel on Constitutional Recognition of Indigenous Australians, *Recognising Aboriginal and Torres Strait Islander Peoples in the Constitution: Report of the Expert Panel*, Report, 16 January 2012, p. 139.
10 *Ibid.*, citing Anne-Marie Mooney Cotter, *Race Matters: An International Legal Analysis of Race Discrimination*, Ashgate, Aldershot, 2006, pp. 6–8.
11 Joint Select Committee on Constitutional Recognition of Aboriginal and Torres Strait Islander Peoples, Parliament of Australia, *Interim Report*, 2014, p. 14.
12 Expert Panel on Constitutional Recognition of Indigenous Australians, *Recognising Aboriginal and Torres Strait Islander Peoples in the Constitution: Report of the Expert Panel*, Report, 16 January 2012, p. xviii; Joint Select Committee on Constitutional Recognition of Aboriginal and Torres Strait Islander Peoples, Parliament of Australia, *Progress Report*, 2014, pp. ix–x.
13 *Racial Discrimination Act 1975* (Cth) section 9.
14 *Mabo v Queensland (No 1) (1988)* 166 Commonwealth Law Reports, p. 186.
15 Expert Panel on Constitutional Recognition of Indigenous Australians, *Recognising Aboriginal and Torres Strait Islander Peoples in the Constitution: Report of the Expert Panel*, Report, 16 January 2012, 'Executive Summary', p. xviii.
16 Patricia Karvelas, 'Historic Constitution Vote over Indigenous Recognition Facing Hurdles', *The Australian* (online), 20 January 2012, <www.theaustralian.com.au/national-affairs/policy/historic-

constitution-vote-over-indigenous-recognition-facing-hurdles/story-fn9hm1pm-1226248879375>.

17 Dennis Shanahan and Paul Kelly, 'Bill of Rights Would Kill Referendum, Says Tony Abbott', *The Australian* (online), 6 September 2014, <www.theaustralian.com.au/national-affairs/indigenous/ bill-of-rights-would-kill-referendum-says-tony-abbott/story- fn9hm1pm-1227049647580>.

18 Joint Select Committee on Constitutional Recognition of Aboriginal and Torres Strait Islander Peoples, Parliament of Australia, *Interim Report*, 2014, p. 11.

19 Expert Panel on Constitutional Recognition of Indigenous Australians, *Recognising Aboriginal and Torres Strait Islander Peoples in the Constitution: Report of the Expert Panel*, 2012, p. xviii.

20 *Ibid.*, p. 131.

6 – The Referendum Council and Uluru process

1 *Statement presented by Aboriginal and Torres Strait Islander attendees at a meeting held today with the Prime Minister and Opposition Leader on Constitutional Recognition*, 6 July 2015, Kirribilli (Sydney), <antar.org.au/sites/default/files/187s1033.pdf>.

2 Referendum Council, *Final Report of the Referendum Council*, 30 June 2017, <www.referendumcouncil.org.au/sites/default/files/report_attachments/Referendum_Council_Final_Report.pdf>, pp. 46–47.

3 Referendum Council, *Final Report of the Referendum Council*, 30 June 2017, <www.referendumcouncil.org.au/sites/default/files/report_attachments/Referendum_Council_Final_Report.pdf>, p. 22.

4 NITV, '"We Won't Sell Out Our Mob": Delegates Walk Out of Constitutional Recognition Forum in Protest', <www.sbs.com.au/nitv/nitv-news/article/2017/05/25/breaking-delegates-walk-out-constitutional-recognition-forum-protest>, 25 May 2017.

5 Referendum Council, *Final Report of the Referendum Council*, 30 June 2017, <www.referendumcouncil.org.au/sites/default/files/report_attachments/Referendum_Council_Final_Report.pdf>, p. 33.

6 *Ibid.*, p. 11.

7 *Ibid.*, p. 109.

8 *Ibid.*, p. 2.

7 – Voice, Makarrata Commission and Truth

1 Anne Twomey, 'Why an Indigenous Voice Would Not Be a "Third Chamber" of Parliament', *Sydney Morning Herald*, 28 May 2019, <www.smh.com.au/national/why-an-indigenous-voice-would-not-be-third-chamber-of-parliament-20190526-p51r7t.html?js-chunk-not-found-refresh=true>.

2 Referendum Council, *Final Report of the Referendum Council*, 30 June 2017, <www.referendumcouncil.org.au/sites/default/files/report_attachments/Referendum_Council_Final_Report.pdf>, p. 2.

3 Murray Gleeson, 'Recognition in Keeping with the Constitution: A Worthwhile Project' (2019), <cdn.brandfolder.io/3RTTK3BV/as/putr90-7ew1ns-5sgfef/Indigenous_Recognition_-_Murray_Gleeson.pdf>, p. 12.
4 Referendum Council, *Final Report of the Referendum Council*, 30 June 2017, <www.referendumcouncil.org.au/sites/default/files/report_attachments/Referendum_Council_Final_Report.pdf>, pp. 30–31.
5 *Ibid.*, p. 14.
6 Referendum Council, *Final Report of the Referendum Council*, 30 June 2017, <www.referendumcouncil.org.au/sites/default/files/report_attachments/Referendum_Council_Final_Report.pdf>, p. 21.
7 *Ibid.*, p. 18.

8 – Responses to the Uluru Statement

1 The Hon. Malcolm Turnbull MP Prime Minister, Senator The Hon. George Brandis QC Attorney-General, Senator The Hon. Nigel Scullion Minister for Indigenous Affairs, 'Joint Press Release: Response to Referendum Council's report on Constitutional Reform', 26 October 2017, <www.malcolmturnbull.com.au/media/response-to-referendum-councils-report-on-constitutional-recognition>.
2 Liberal Party of Australia, 'Our Plan to Support Indigenous Australians', 15 May 2019, <apo.org.au/sites/default/files/resource-files/2019-05/apo-nid242236.pdf>.
3 Parliament of the Commonwealth of Australia, Joint Select Committee on Constitutional Recognition relating to Aboriginal and Torres Strait Islander Peoples, *Final Report* (November 2018), Recommendation 1, p. xvii.
4 *Ibid.*
5 Ken Wyatt, 'A Voice for Indigenous Australians', Media Release, 30 October 2019, ministers.pmc.gov.au/wyatt/2019/voice-indigenous-australians>.
6 Ken Wyatt, 'National Press Club Address – Walking in Partnership to Effect Change', Speech, 10 July 2019, <ministers.pmc.gov.au/wyatt/2019/national-press-club-address-walking-partnership-effect-change>.
7 Ken Wyatt, 'Voice Co-Design Underway', Media Release, 13 November 2019, <www.indigenous.gov.au/Voice%20CoDesign%20Underway>.
8 Scott Morrison, 'Address, Closing the Gap Statement to Parliament', Speech, 12 February 2020, <www.pm.gov.au/media/address-closing-gap-statement-parliament>.
9 BR Wise, *The Making of the Australian Commonwealth, 1889–1900*, Longmans Green, London, 1913, p. 356.
10 This text includes an extract from the International Court of Justice in its Advisory Opinion on Western Sahara (62) (1975) ICJ Rep, [85]–[86], quoted in *Mabo v Queensland [No 2]* (1992) 175 CLR 1 [40].
11 Anne Twomey, 'Why an Indigenous Voice Would Not Be a 'Third Chamber' of Parliament', *Sydney Morning Herald*, 28 May 2019, <www.smh.com.

au/national/why-an-indigenous-voice-would-not-be-third-chamber-of-parliament-20190526-p51r7t.html>.
12 *Canada Act 1982* (UK) c 11, sch B, section 35(1).
13 Constitution of Norway (1814) article 110a.
14 Constitution of Finland (1999) section 17.

9 – Yes to the Voice?

1 Reconciliation Australia, 'Reconciliation Support Grows But More Needs to be Done – Latest Australian Reconciliation Barometer', 11 February 2019, <www.reconciliation.org.au/reconciliation-support-grows-but-more-needs-to-be-done-latest-australian-reconciliation-barometer/>.
2 F Markham and W Sanders, *Support for a Constitutionally Enshrined First Nations Voice to Parliament: Evidence from Opinion Research since 2017* (Centre for Aboriginal Economic Policy Research, 2020), p. 22.
3 Reconciliation Australia, '2021 State of Reconciliation in Australia', <www.reconciliation.org.au/wp-content/uploads/2021/01/state-of-reconciliation-2021-full-report_web.pdf>.
4 Australian Electoral Commission, *1999 Referendum*, 24 January 2011, <www.aec.gov.au/elections/referendums/1999_referendum_reports_statistics/index.htm>.
5 George Williams, Sean Brennan and Andrew Lynch, *Australian Constitutional Law and Theory: Commentary and Materials*, Federation Press, Sydney, 6th edition, 2014, pp. 1339–1340.
6 George Williams and David Hume, *People Power: The History and Future of the Referendum in Australia*, UNSW Press, Sydney, 2010.

INDEX